THE CAREER REINVENTION BLUEPRINT™

From Restless to Realigned – 7 steps to finding work that fits and a life that matters

Dr David Onu

PRAISE FOR THE CAREER REINVENTION BLUEPRINT™

'Practical, inspiring, contemporary, comprehensive, easy to follow, and grounded in real experiences – this book offers a clear roadmap for anyone seeking meaningful career reinvention, with insights that resonate across almost every career. I strongly recommend it to anyone seeking career reinvention.'

– PROFESSOR ADULI E.O. MALAU-ADULI, PhD FRSN, Editor-in-Chief, *Australian Journal of Agricultural, Veterinary and Animal Sciences*

'This book is more than just words on a page. It's a mirror that helps you recognize the difference between being merely tired and being truly called to grow. The idea of seeing discomfort as a compass helped me navigate the toughest period of my life – the loss of my dear wife. It gave me clarity, strength, and a sense of direction when everything felt uncertain. If you're searching for insight and courage to move forward through life's hardest moments, or if you've ever felt stuck or restless without knowing why, this book will give you the clarity to see your struggle in a new light and the courage to move forward. Endowed with 'Clarity of Purpose', it balances storytelling with science and inspiration, garnished with practical frameworks.'

– PHILIP UDEH, Business Administrator, Ministry of Justice, UK

'It felt as though the author had seen the very events of my life and put them into words. Not every book opens you up. But *The Career Reinvention Blueprint™* did that for me. It spoke directly to my soul and revealed truths I didn't know I was carrying. Sometimes, the very identity that once built and defined your success becomes the same box that traps you in. This book gave me permission to pause, reflect, and reinvent – to evolve into a more purposeful and fulfilled version of myself.'

— PHARM CHIDIMMA OBI, Cancer Advocate, Nigeria

'I first trained as a mechanical engineer to fulfil my father's wish before pursuing my own dream as a geoscientist. *The Career Reinvention Blueprint™* captures that very journey of breaking tradition to design one's own identity. It offers practical guidance on building a support system that fuels your growth as you pivot. This masterpiece is a compelling and inspiring read.'

— DR CHARLES MAKOUNDI, PhD, Senior Adjunct Researcher, University of Tasmania, Australia

'Remarkable! Dr Onu has told his story profoundly, with some hard truths, but in a practical way that helps you live a purposeful life without losing yourself. Success without fulfillment can be frustrating; this book will undoubtedly help you have your cake and eat it, too. It's the missing piece of life everyone should read and navigate.'

– FELIX OBASI, Registered Nurse, NHS, UK

'This book is the encouragement you need to get yourself out of the ordinary and into the extraordinary. It offers not only practical advice but also invitations for self-reflection, providing good examples of how people have changed their lives for the better. I found the book to be easily absorbed and highly relatable. I felt like the author was writing directly to me, as I had many 'ah-ha' moments. I highly recommend this book to anyone seeking more from their lives.'

– CLARE GLADE-WRIGHT, Deputy Mayor of Kingborough, Tasmania

'I thoroughly enjoyed *The Career Reinvention Blueprint*™! This book is a comprehensive guide for anyone looking to transform their career and find purpose. The insights and strategies are practical, relatable, and inspiring. What resonated with me most was the emphasis on self-reflection, exploration, and intentional decision-making. Whether you're feeling stuck, seeking a career change, or simply looking to grow, this book is a must-read. Highly recommended.'

– NDIUKWU EZINNE CHIOMA, Director, Marriage Insights

'Dr Onu asks some uncomfortable and thought-provoking questions, speaking directly to the restless parts of your mind, all done with his trademark warmth, kindness, and passion.'

– ROB SKINNER, Hospitality Industry Leader, Tasmania.

'Reading *The Career Reinvention Blueprint*™ reminded me of my own journey. After becoming financially independent, I left my role as an NHS GP to spend more time with my young family and create my first business. But once the dust settled, I too felt that quiet restlessness Dr Onu describes so well – the sense that success and freedom aren't the same as purpose. The *7-step framework* and the *P.A.R.N. method* provide a practical roadmap, while the stories of global leaders he shared show what reinvention can really look like. Reinvention is not about throwing away your past; it's about realigning with who you're becoming. Everyone at a crossroads should read this.'

– DR NDUBUISI 'ANDY' EGWIM, former NHS GP and Founder, MoneyWise Doctor.

"Dr. David Onu did an amazing job putting this book together. As someone who has personally walked the path of career reinvention, I can confidently say this isn't just theory — it's a powerful guide that speaks to real experiences and bold transitions. Career Reinvention Blueprint™ is packed with clarity, strategy, and practical steps to help you make your next move with confidence. You need to read this!"

– FAITH RACHEAL OGUNDEYI, Registered Nurse & Expert Writer, Nigeria.

FROM RESTLESS TO REALIGNED

THE CAREER REINVENTION BLUEPRINT™

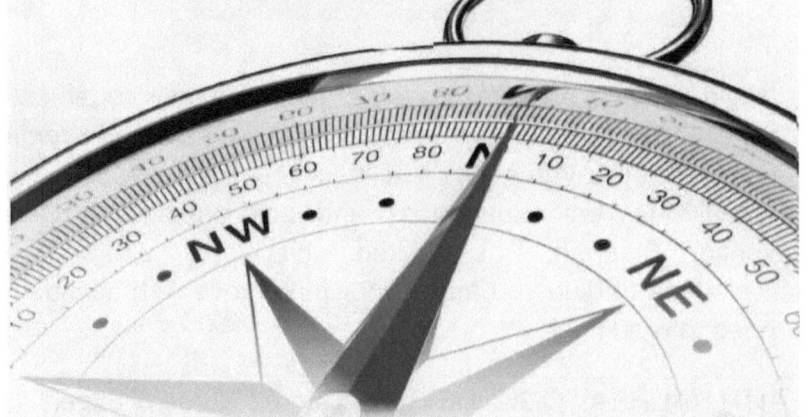

7 STEPS TO FINDING WORK THAT FITS AND A LIFE THAT MATTERS

DR. DAVID ONU

Foreword by Dr. Ikechukwu Okoh

First published in 2025 by Grow & Lead Press

© Dr David Onu 2025

The moral rights of the author have been asserted.

The Career Reinvention Blueprint™

From Restless to Realigned – 7 steps to finding work that fits and a life that matters.

All rights reserved, including rights for text and data mining and training of artificial intelligence technologies or similar technologies. Except as permitted under the *Australian Copyright Act 1968* or other similar laws (for example, a fair dealing for the purposes of study, research, criticism or reviews), no part of this publication may be reproduced or transmitted by any person or entity, in any form or by any means – electronic or mechanical, including photocopying, recording, scanning or by any information storage and retrieval system or otherwise, without prior written permission of the author.

ISBN: 978-1-7642714-2-4

www.careerreinventionblueprint.com I www.davidonu.com

A catalogue record for this book is available from the National Library of Australia

The Career Reinvention Blueprint™ is a trademark of Dr David Onu. All other trademarks are the property of their respective owners.

This book is intended for educational and inspirational purposes only. The author and publisher disclaim liability for any loss of profit or any other commercial damages, including but not limited to special, incidental, consequential, or any other damages, personal or otherwise, incurred as a direct or indirect use and application of any information contained herein.

To My Family

To my wife, Chinyere, and children – Zoronachi, Chidiamara, Olaedo, and Nneoma – you are my reason for pressing pause, my courage to choose differently, and my compass toward what truly matters. Every page of this book carries the imprint of your laughter and love.

To The Reader

And to every individual standing at the crossroads of work and life, restless or misaligned, and quietly wondering, *"Is there more for me?"* – this book is for you. You are not late, not lost, but right on time for your next chapter.

FOREWORD

At some point in every career, a quiet restlessness sets in. You have achieved significant milestones and earned the respect of your peers, yet something within whispers, *"Is this really it?"* That tension between success and fulfillment is not a flaw; it is a signal. And that is why this book is essential.

In **The Career Reinvention Blueprint™,** Dr David Onu speaks directly to those standing at life's crossroads. He understands the struggle at first hand.

Once a surgeon with prestige and stability, David made the bold decision to step away from the well-trodden path and pursue a life that truly resonated with him. That choice was not easy, but it brought him what many secretly yearn for: **clarity, freedom, and alignment**.

What distinguishes this book is its honesty. It does not pretend that reinvention is effortless, nor does it romanticise quitting. Instead, it offers a **practical 7-step roadmap**, grounded in lived experiences and real client stories, as well as valuable tools. Along the way, you'll encounter the journeys of remarkable leaders and professionals from around the world. Their stories don't stand apart – they flow as living proof of this method in action. Each one demonstrates how these seven steps are applied in real life, various contexts, and lead to lasting transformation.

Whether you are a young professional sensing that there is more to life ahead, a mid-life leader feeling the weight of misalignment, someone on a non-professional path, or a retiree seeking renewed purpose, these pages will offer relatable insights.

As you read, be prepared to pause, reflect, and realign. You'll encounter thought-provoking questions, discover new possibilities, and most importantly, gain permission to redefine success on your own terms. This book is timely. We live in an era of widespread burnout, yet the hunger for meaningful work has never been stronger. What Dr Onu offers here is not just hope, but a tangible path forward.

My encouragement is simple: do not merely read this book, engage with it. Journal alongside it. Discuss it with others. Let it guide your next steps, however small they may be.

Reinvention rarely begins with giant leaps; it starts with a single honest decision.

Dr Onu has provided you with a blueprint. The rest is in your hands. Please find the courage in these pages to move from restlessness to realignment, and create not just a career that works, but a life that matters.

Dr Ikechukwu Okoh

Medical Specialist, Executive Coach, and Group Head at Boulevard Group, UK

Connect with him at: https://linkedin.com/in/ikechukwu-dominic-okoh

CONTENTS

PRAISE FOR THE CAREER REINVENTION BLUEPRINT™ II

FOREWORD IX

CONTENTS XI

WELCOME: MY STORY, AND WHY I WROTE THIS BOOK XIV

INTRODUCTION: SUCCESS ISN'T ALWAYS ENOUGH – RECOGNIZE THE RESTLESSNESS WITHIN YOU XXII

PART 1 XXVI

THE BLUEPRINT: THE 7 STEPS OF REINVENTION XXVI

CHAPTER 1: IDENTIFY YOUR TRUE DISCOMFORT – ARE YOU TIRED OR READY TO GROW? 1

CHAPTER 2: ADOPT AN EXPANSIVE MINDSET – BREAK FREE FROM YOUR LIMITING BELIEFS 16

CHAPTER 3: DEFINE YOUR DESTINATION CLEARLY – KNOWING EXACTLY WHERE YOU'RE HEADED 34

CHAPTER 4: SELECT YOUR PATH WISELY – DECIDE BETWEEN A QUIET PIVOT AND A BOLD LEAP 52

CHAPTER 5: BUILD A SUPPORT CIRCLE – WHY REINVENTION THRIVES ON CONNECTION 66

CHAPTER 6: NAVIGATE CULTURAL, SOCIETAL, AND FAMILY EXPECTATIONS – REINVENT WITHOUT GUILT OR REGRET 78

CHAPTER 7: OVERCOME THE HIDDEN COST OF SUCCESS – PRIORITISE YOUR HEALTH, FAMILY, AND FULFILLMENT 90

PART 2 104

THE STORIES – REAL JOURNEYS OF REINVENTION 104

CHAPTER 8: FROM INTENSIVE CARE TO FREEDOM – DR OLA VAN STEEN'S JOURNEY 105

CHAPTER 9: FROM A HOUSEBOY TO A GLOBAL INFLUENCER – DR IFEANYI AKALEME'S BECOMING 120

CHAPTER 10: FROM STAY-AT-HOME MUM TO GLOBAL INFLUENCE – EMILY WALE-KOYA'S JOURNEY 131

PART 3 139

THE FUTURE – LIVING AND LEAVING A LEGACY 139

CHAPTER 11: LEGACY BEYOND RETIREMENT – REINVENTING FOR PURPOSE AND IMPACT 140

CAREER REINVENTION TOOLKIT – PRACTICAL STEPS TO ALIGN YOUR LIFE AND CAREER 150

ACKNOWLEDGEMENTS 158

ABOUT THE AUTHOR 161

LET'S KEEP WALKING THIS PATH TOGETHER 165

WELCOME: MY STORY, AND WHY I WROTE THIS BOOK

"True leadership isn't about being strong all the time. It's about knowing when to pause, reflect, and realign with your values."

– Dr David Onu

I'm Dr David Onu.

If you had met me more than a decade ago, you would have thought I had it all figured out.

I was a surgeon – respected, well-paid, climbing the professional ladder. I was constantly in motion and burning the candle at both ends.

The path appeared clear, prestigious, and predictable.

From the outside, it looked like success. But inside, I felt an ever-growing distance between the career which had been my dream, and the rest of my life including my family and my duties as a father.

The Shift That Changed Everything

The breaking point came when my wife was eight months pregnant. We had relocated to Australia just a year earlier, and we had no family nearby, no built-in support system. She was struggling to keep up with the demands of her pregnancy while also caring for our one-year-old firstborn son. I was struggling too, though for very different reasons. My wife needed her husband, my sons – born and unborn – needed their father, but my career left no room for me to be present.

Days in the hospital blurred into nights, marked by endless on-call rotations, marathon theatre sessions, and the pursuit of one goal after another, culminating in full registration by the Australian Medical Board and permanent residency.

And all the while, my unborn son kicked inside my wife, a small but urgent reminder that time was running out.

Then came the quiet, unsettling questions I could no longer push aside:

- What is the cost of my career?
- Will my kids truly know their dad?
- Is success still success if it destroys my health and my marriage?
- What if the person I've worked so hard to become isn't the person I'm meant to be anymore?

The hardest part wasn't choosing a new path.

It was stepping away from the well-paved road, especially when, on paper, it made perfect sense to stay.

I wrestled with fear, self-doubt, and that sharp, haunting thought: "What will people say if I walk away from all of this?"

At that difficult moment, the wise words of Gary Chapman echoed in my head:

> *"I realize now that life is short, and we are very foolish if we do not keep a balance between work and family. If in trying to be a success, you lose your wife and family, you've lost it all."*

So, I made a move that changed everything. I asked for one month off.

One month to breathe.

One month to think without the relentless beeping of hospital monitors in the background.

One month to listen to my heart and clear my fogged-up head.

It was, without question, the hardest decision of my professional life.

Pressing pause on a career I had spent years building felt like betrayal – not just of my profession, but of the version of me who had fought tooth and nail to get here.

And yet, in that pause, I discovered something far more precious: a deeper purpose – one that encompassed both my passion and my family.

I hadn't lost my ambition. I had simply outgrown the box I was in.

That was when I applied what I later learned to be the **Corridor Principle**:

> *Doors don't open before you move – they open because you moved. So, you have to make the bold move. It's only then that you see the next door.*

The truth is, sometimes the most respected paths are the ones that feel most restrictive. And the very identity that built your success can quietly become the box that traps you.

For years, I was a high achiever but quietly unfulfilled: not because the field of medicine failed me, but because I had outgrown the version of me who chose it.

From Doctor to Something More

Many years after I left my surgical career, a simple question cracked me wide open one night:

> *"What if there's more for me, and I'm allowed to explore it?"*

I didn't know it at the time, but that question significantly changed my perspective.

For a long time, my identity was closely tied to being a medical doctor. It was who I was, not just what I did.

But over time, I realised I could honour my profession without being confined by it.

In the last three and a half years, I've expanded my life beyond the field of medicine.

I've become a community builder and mentored others on their transformative journeys.

I've started a blog, become a storyteller, and received training as a Results, Relationship, Life, and Career Reinvention Coach.

I didn't do any of these because I stopped loving medicine as a field, but because I started loving the fuller version of my life.

Here's what I've learned: reinvention isn't about erasing your past, it's about building a life that finally fits who you're becoming.

Why I Wrote This Book and Why it Deserves Your Full Attention

Many people feel stuck in a life that no longer suits them, but don't know how to make a change.

They feel guilty for wanting more. Or afraid they've missed their moment.

Some don't even have the words for what's wrong. They just know something doesn't feel right anymore.

Sound familiar?

This book was born not only from my lived experiences, but also from the stories of the people I've worked with.

You'll encounter inspiring individuals throughout this book, like Dr Ola van Steen, who pivoted from the high-pressure world of intensive and acute medical care to build a thriving global travel enterprise. Her journey is a vivid reminder that reinvention is possible at any stage of life.

To protect their identities, the names of my clients featured in this book have been changed.

I wrote this book because I know the fear of letting go of the known. I've been there.

I know what it's like to stand at the crossroads between duty and desire, between the life you've built and the life that's calling you.

And I know the courage it takes to take that first step, especially when you can't see the whole map.

My mission now is simple: to help you get clear, build courage, and take the steps that will lead you to work that fits and a life that matters.

- Maybe you're here because you're curious.
- Maybe you're here because you're tired.
- Or maybe you're here because you're ready.

Wherever you are, I want you to know this:

You don't have to have it all figured out to begin. Just start walking. The doors will appear and open for you.

Who This Book is For

Whether you are:

- An early-career professional wondering, "What's next?"
- A successful mid-life leader who feels strangely restless.
- A person who is running a business, or not on a set career path, but still hungry for growth.

➢ A retiree seeking purpose beyond a well-earned rest…

This book is for you.

I've coached people at every stage of their journey, and one of the many things I've realized is that reinvention isn't just for people in crisis. It's for anyone brave enough to ask, "Is there more?"

Note: This book is broadly applicable to all career paths, both professional and non-professional.

What You'll Get From This Book

This isn't just a book to read; it's a blueprint to walk you through your **Career Reinvention** journey, a gentle hand on your shoulder when you're unsure of your next step.

I wrote it to be clear and practical. Not filled with unrealistic promises, but grounded help for people who are asking life's honest questions.

Inside, you will find:

➢ Clarity for your first or next career move.

➢ A way forward from burnout to purpose.

➢ Practical tools for career reinvention.

➢ Guidance in turning your life experience into fresh opportunities.

Imagine waking up one Monday morning with clarity about your next step, courage to pursue it, and the confidence that your work now reflects your deeper values. This is the life on the other side of restlessness – and it's possible for you.

You don't need to have it all figured out. You just need a starting point. That's what this book gives you.

I'm Dr David Onu, Career Reinvention Coach and Leadership Mentor, here to help you move from restless to realigned.

Before we begin, I want to share an important note regarding the content of this book.

Content Warning

This book contains descriptions of many distressing experiences, including trauma, adversity, abject poverty, rejection, job loss, bullying, deaths, and intense emotional and psychological challenges. Some readers may find these sections emotionally difficult or triggering.

We acknowledge and respect the diverse experiences and identities of all readers. If you find any content distressing, please consider seeking support from a trusted health professional, counsellor, or helpline. Your wellbeing is essential.

INTRODUCTION: SUCCESS ISN'T ALWAYS ENOUGH – RECOGNIZE THE RESTLESSNESS WITHIN YOU

"There is no greater agony than bearing an untold story inside you."

– Maya Angelou

I had already paid the price to become a brain surgeon. Years of study, sleepless nights, countless exams, and gruelling training will eventually pay off – or so I thought.

But here's the hidden truth about dreams: sometimes they fit you perfectly at one stage of life, only to start suffocating you at another.

At first, the whispers were faint, those quiet moments driving home after long night shifts, wondering, "Is this really it?" But those whispers grew louder until they became an ache I could no longer ignore.

In 2012, I made my first bold pivot, a significant leap away from surgery, leaving behind the identity I had built over the previous decade.

And more recently came my second reinvention: a slower, more deliberate shift into blogging, writing, storytelling, coaching, and thought leadership, all while continuing to practice medicine.

What this journey taught me is powerful: you can have success and still feel restless. You can check every box and still sense another life quietly calling your name.

This book is about that restlessness inside you; how to recognize it, listen to it, and find work and a life that fits who you're becoming, not just who you have been.

You Might Be in That Space Right Now

If you've ever sat in your car after work, hands on the wheel, staring into space because something inside feels unsettled, welcome. You're holding the exact book you need right now.

You are doing the right things, but deep down, something no longer feels right. You're tired, not just outwardly, but there's a quiet misalignment within.

You feel off-course, even if you can't yet say what it is. You've probably started to wonder whether your current life reflects your evolving values and your deeper purpose.

You're ready for something more meaningful, something that truly fits who you've grown to be. However, perhaps you're unsure about how to make the pivot.

If you're thinking, "That's me", you're not alone. You're one of a growing number of people feeling the same way.

According to a Gallup study, only 15% of people globally feel truly engaged in their work. That means 85% are going through the motions: restless, misaligned, and quietly wondering if there's another way.

This book is your companion in answering that restlessness. It was born from my lived experience and those conversations, the ones I've had over the years with professionals, leaders, students, and everyday people at a crossroads.

These are people who felt like they were meant for more but didn't quite know how to go about it, until they finally broke through after our sessions together.

Here's what I want you to know: reinvention doesn't start with a résumé. It begins with reflection. So, this is an invitation to pause, reflect, and realign with what truly matters.

And from that place of honest reflection, you can begin to build a path forward, one that genuinely feels like you.

This book will guide you through that journey, step by step, using my personal story, real-life examples, grounded research, and clear exercises to help you move from feeling stuck and restless to becoming realigned and finding work that fits, and a life that matters.

As you work through this blueprint, you'll move from restless to realigned – finding not just a career that fits, but a renewed sense of clarity, confidence, and fulfillment in life.

A Pause Before We Begin

Before you dive into this blueprint, take a breath and answer these questions:

- What's your current sense of fulfillment?
- Where do you feel that quiet restlessness nudging you?

I know you may not have the answers yet. Just be honest with yourself, that's where reinvention starts.

So, go ahead and turn the page. We'll figure this out together. Happy reading!

PART 1

THE BLUEPRINT: THE 7 STEPS OF REINVENTION

Every transformation begins with awareness – the quiet moment you admit there's more to life than this.

CHAPTER 1: IDENTIFY YOUR TRUE DISCOMFORT – ARE YOU TIRED OR READY TO GROW?

"Awareness is the first step for meaningful transformation."

– Dr David Onu

Have you ever found yourself sitting in silence, staring at your computer or phone, unsure of why you're feeling so off, yet knowing deep down that something isn't right?

That subtle discomfort isn't just stress. It's not just exhaustion. It's your inner self trying to get your attention.

This is where career reinvention begins. Not with a resignation letter or a business plan – but with **awareness**.

Before you can **realign**, you must recognize where you've **misaligned**. Before you pivot, you must acknowledge that you're stuck. And before you **reinvent**, you must become deeply honest about **what no longer fits**. (I want you to reread this until it becomes rooted in your heart.)

Awareness Is Your Awakening

It's the moment you stop running on autopilot.

The moment you admit to yourself, "I don't think I'm happy here anymore." Or, "I've outgrown this version of my life."

Most of the time, it's not dramatic. It might even feel quiet at first, like a whisper.

A sacred whisper, more like a nudge and a desire for something more meaningful, a drive for **more**.

Sometimes, we dismiss that whisper because it is our own.

Ralph Waldo Emerson said this:

> "A man should learn to detect and watch that gleam of light which flashes across his mind from within, more than the lustre of the firmament of bards and sages. Yet he dismisses without notice his thought, because it is his."

And oftentimes, we dismiss our inner voice because it's inconvenient.

We tell ourselves:

- I should be grateful.
- Others have it worse.
- Maybe I'm just tired.
- Let me give it one more year.

However, awareness doesn't disappear when ignored; instead, it deepens.

3 | THE CAREER REINVENTION BLUEPRINT™

I had ignored this same awareness before my first pivot from being a surgeon, but the more I ignored it, the deeper it became.

It showed up in new ways: a lack of energy, a short fuse, a restlessness I couldn't explain, a discomfort that no weekend getaway or promotion could fix.

Perhaps I'm painting a picture of your current phase, and that is to show you that you're not alone. I was once in your current state.

And every client I've worked with – founders, professionals, creatives, and leaders – has also reached a point where the life they built no longer felt aligned with who they were becoming.

Their reinvention didn't begin with a new opportunity. It started with being aware of what wasn't working anymore.

So ask yourself:

- When did I last feel excited about my work?
- Is what I'm doing today still aligned with who I am now?
- Am I living someone else's version of success, or my own?

These questions are not easy. But they are necessary to start your reinvention journey.

This chapter is about being honest with yourself. Not in order to make sudden changes, but to pause and identify your actual discomfort.

To start with, let go of the pressure to figure everything out at once. For now, just listen to the restlessness inside you.

Observe and notice what no longer feels right. Let that discomfort be your compass to your next chapter, not your enemy.

Three Steps to Transformation

1. Awareness of the Problem

Awareness is not the whole journey. But without it, no genuine reinvention is possible. This is your moment of clarity, your permission to say, "Something has to shift, and I'm ready to begin."

2. Acceptance of What Is or Will Be (Steps You'll Take)

Accept the reality of your current situation and the changes that are required ahead. This is where you begin to decide on the steps you'll take to move forward.

3. Appreciation for Your Journey

Tap into the wisdom from your past, value the lessons learned, and embrace the person you're becoming.

As you turn these pages, know that we're walking this journey together, step by step, toward the change you've been longing for.

Trapped Inside a Perspex Box

A former client, I'll call Michelle, a mid-level professional, once told me she felt like she was "trapped inside a box."

From the outside, everything looked ideal. She earned a handsome income, enjoyed high status, and had the admiration of her colleagues and family.

But inside, she was quietly suffering, feeling confined by the very success she had worked so diligently to achieve.

She couldn't explain it at first, but her work felt increasingly meaningless. It wasn't merely fatigue or burnout; it was a deeper signal urging her towards growth and alignment.

Through our coaching sessions, Michelle began to realize she'd been living out a version of success that wasn't truly her own. Her path had been shaped more by external validation and societal expectations than by inner conviction.

Together, we began peeling back the layers of her discontent: gently, honestly, and without judgment.

Sometimes, the life you built no longer fits the person you've become. And that is perfectly fine.

Two Types of Discomfort: Which One Are You Feeling?

Before you leap into change, it's essential to understand the kind of discomfort you're feeling because not all restlessness means it's time to quit your job.

Sometimes, it just means it's time to pause and realign.

I will break this down into the two significant types of discomfort described in the **Two-factor Theory** developed by psychologist Frederick Herzberg.

Herzberg's Motivation–Hygiene Theory

Motivators

 Achievement
 Recognition
 The Work Itself
 Responsibility
 Growth

Hygiene Factors

 Bureaucracy (Corporate policies, Supervision)
 Relationships
 Status
 Salary
 Job Security

HERZBERG'S TWO-FACTOR OUTCOMES

Hygiene Factors (vertical axis) / *Motivation Factors* (horizontal axis, Low → High)

Comfortable but unfulfilling
Stable, low engagement

Fun and exciting
High energy & satisfaction

Miserable job
Low morale, turnover risk

Hard but meaningful
Challenging with purpose

1. Situational Discomfort

Also known as **Hygiene** factors, these discomforts are like wearing a heavy coat in the sun. It's suffocating, yes, but your environment, not your essence, causes them. Once the sun sets or the coat comes off, relief returns.

These factors include supervision at work, relationships with your supervisor, company policies, compensation, and job security.

As Herzberg observed:

> *"Adequate hygiene factors decrease job dissatisfaction, but by themselves do not create strong satisfaction."*

You might be in situational discomfort if:

- You still enjoy the core of your work but feel undervalued, overworked, or burned out.
- Your stress rises and falls depending on the work season, your workload, or your boss.
- A weekend getaway or break from work helps you breathe again.
- You feel like yourself once the work pressure lifts.

In this space, you're burned out, but not broken. Your spark of passion remains, but is buried under temporary challenges.

Sometimes, however, even when you leave the difficult situation, its emotional weight lingers.

A client of mine experienced this deeply after working under a controlling boss in a toxic environment.

She shared, "I thought I was going crazy". Though she had left the job, the trauma followed her for months, and feeling controlled, belittled, and micromanaged left her constantly on edge.

Even in a healthier environment, she found herself over-explaining her decisions, avoiding leadership roles, and feeling unsafe with feedback, regardless of how kindly it was given.

I reassured her, "You're not going crazy. You're healing from something real – what I call **Post-Traumatic Boss Disorder (PTBS)**." Though not a clinical term, PTBS captures how toxic leadership can leave lasting scars, echoing in your mind long after you've walked away. It's a metaphor, not a medical term – but for many, it names the invisible weight they've been carrying.

Recognizing this was her turning point, the start of rebuilding confidence, setting healthy boundaries, and learning to trust herself again.

Ever felt this way? Sometimes the answer isn't a complete career reinvention but a thoughtful restructuring.

It might mean setting firmer boundaries, asking for support, or simply taking a well-deserved break to recharge.

2. Growth Discomfort

The sources of growth discomfort, also known as **Motivation** factors, are entirely different. This discomfort doesn't fade with time off work or a change in scenery, rather it usually deepens because it touches your core needs.

According to Herzberg:

> "Motivators – achievement, recognition, the work itself, advancement, growth – are intrinsic to the job and lead

> *to job satisfaction because they satisfy the human needs for growth and self-actualization."*

Unlike Hygiene factors, Motivators drive engagement and fulfillment. To reach higher levels of satisfaction and genuine engagement, organizations must provide strong Motivators.

You might be feeling growth discomfort if:

- ➤ You're deeply competent, but no longer curious.

- ➤ Your work pays well, but your heart isn't in it.

- ➤ You crave meaning and impact more than status or milestones.

- ➤ You've constantly asked yourself, "What if there's more for me and I'm allowed to explore it?"

This kind of unrest isn't a flaw; it's a sign. **It was my sign**.

According to research published in the *Journal of Vocational Behavior*, career dissatisfaction often arises not just from job-related stress, but from a misalignment between **personal values** and **professional roles**.

When your inner world evolves, but your outer world doesn't shift with it, discontent becomes a chronic condition.

It's like a plant that's outgrown its pot. You can water it all you want, but until it's replanted in richer soil, with more room to expand, it can't thrive.

So, which discomfort are you feeling?

Are you tired, or truly ready to grow?

The Science of Growth: Mindset Matters

Research by psychologist Carol Dweck highlights the power of mindset, particularly distinguishing between a **Fixed** and a **Growth mindset**.

People with a fixed mindset believe their abilities and intelligence are static. They avoid challenges for fear of failure.

But people with a growth mindset are the opposite: they believe they can evolve, adapt, and grow through effort and learning.

We will be exploring the different mindsets and Carol Dweck's work in more detail in the next chapter.

Michelle (the client I talked about earlier) had her breakthrough following our coaching sessions; she stopped seeing her career as a static identity and started seeing it as a journey.

She shifted from "This is who I am" to "This is who I was – but who I become is up to me."

So much reinvention starts with this mindset shift.

Are You Betraying Your Calling, or Answering It?

One of the most common fears people express when it comes to career reinvention is this:

> *"I've spent years building this. Am I betraying all that effort if I walk away now?"*

But what if leaving isn't betrayal?

Remember: reinvention doesn't always mean burning bridges; sometimes, it's just a quiet shift into a new direction and a new chapter.

You can honour what has brought you this far, while building a future that truly aligns with who you are becoming.

You're not throwing away your past. You're bringing it with you as experience, as wisdom, and as seasoning for the next version of you.

When I pivoted into a new career path, I didn't leave my medical degree or years of experience behind. They became the foundation and an added advantage to the latest version of me.

On the other hand, Michelle didn't discard her law degree or her extensive experience. She kept what she loved, dropped what drained her, and fully embraced the person she was becoming.

Reinvention doesn't mean **letting go of everything**. It means **redirection**.

How to Identify Your Discomfort

You can't fix what you haven't faced. And when it comes to career discomfort, most people don't even know where to start looking.

So here's a gentle, practical way to get clearer on what's really going on underneath that restlessness and sacred nudge that may be pointing toward your next chapter.

I call it the **P.A.R.N. Method**: a simple, science-backed way to slow down, get honest, and name what's really happening inside.

The P.A.R.N. Framework

1. P – Pause the Performance

In my work as a Career Reinvention Coach, I've seen how powerful this pause can be in identifying my discomfort or that of my clients. As I described earlier, I took one month off from my demanding job as a surgeon just to pause, listen to my inner restlessness, and clear my fogged-up head.

During that pause, I discovered something far more precious – a deeper purpose, one that encompassed both my passion and my family.

You don't have to pretend that everything is fine. You don't have to smile through it, make excuses, or convince anyone, including yourself, that you're "just in a phase".

You need a space where you can pause and drop the act.

For some, it may be pouring your heart out on a blank page in your journal, describing how you feel, and naming the discomfort you're facing.

It might be taking a long walk listening to your favourite playlist, or having a deep, honest conversation with someone who truly sees you and cares. Someone who has been there.

And that is precisely the space I create for people as a Career Reinvention Coach: a safe, judgment-free space where we focus on what truly matters: your next chapter.

2. A – Ask Better Questions

Forget the cliché question, "Where do you see yourself in five years?" You need soul-stirring, truth-digging questions like:

- What part of my current work brings me joy?

- When do I feel most alive?
- What am I pretending not to know?
- If I weren't afraid, what would I explore?

Research shows that intentional self-assessment, really asking the right questions, can lead to greater career alignment, higher life satisfaction, and more deliberate life choices.

So don't rush your answers. Sit with them and let them speak back to you.

3. R – Reflect on Who You've Become

We evolve, and sometimes, the life we once built no longer fits the person we've become.

Heraclitus, an ancient Greek philosopher, said it this way:

> "No one ever steps in the same river twice, for it's not the same river and he's not the same man."

Take a moment to look back.

- Who were you five years ago?
- What did you want then, and is it still true today?
- Are you still chasing old dreams out of habit, loyalty, or fear?

Self-reflection isn't outdated; it enhances emotional stability and helps you make more informed long-term decisions.

4. N – Name the Feeling

There's power in naming what's been sitting heavy on your heart. When you name what you're feeling, you start to loosen its grip.

Try putting your discomfort into one sentence:

- I feel trapped in predictability and crave meaningful creativity.

- I'm respected, but I don't feel alive.

- I'm doing what I'm good at, but not what I'm called to.

Psychologists refer to this as **affect labelling**, and it has been proven to reduce the feeling of being overwhelmed and bring clarity. But the sentence has to come from your heart, not your résumé.

Remember: Clarity doesn't shout, it whispers. And the only way to hear it is to slow down, lean in, and listen.

Summary

In this chapter, we explored the first step in career reinvention: **identifying your actual discomfort.** You learned that the subtle restlessness you feel isn't just stress or fatigue; it's a signal that something in your life or career no longer fits.

We distinguished between situational discomfort (temporary, environment-driven) and growth discomfort (deep, signalling misalignment with your evolving self). Using the **P.A.R.N.** method: **Pause**, **Ask**, **Reflect**, and **Name**, you discovered practical ways to slow down, face your feelings honestly, and clarify what's truly driving your desire for change.

The key takeaway: your discomfort is not your enemy, it's your compass, guiding you toward a career and life that align with who you are becoming.

In the next chapter (Chapter 2), we'll explore the next step, which is about how adopting an expansive mindset can help you break free from limiting beliefs and open the door to new possibilities for your career growth and reinvention.

Reflective Questions for You

- Is your restlessness a cry for rest, or a call to rise?

- Is it burnout, or is it a signal that you're growing past your current assignment?

- What is your discomfort trying to teach you about who you're becoming?

CHAPTER 2: ADOPT AN EXPANSIVE MINDSET – BREAK FREE FROM YOUR LIMITING BELIEFS

"Your playing small does not serve the world. There is nothing enlightened about shrinking so that others won't feel insecure around you."

– Marianne Williamson.

If there's one chapter in this book you absolutely cannot afford to skim through, it's this one. In fact, I'd go as far as saying, read it slowly, read it twice, and come back to it whenever you feel stuck.

Why? Because your mindset is the engine that drives every reinvention, every transformation, every next step in your career and life.

I believe you've already taken that brave first step: identifying the actual discomfort behind your restlessness, just as we explored in Chapter 1. Now, it's time for the next decisive step to the bigger life you've been longing for.

In this chapter, we'll discuss and explore:

- ➤ What an expansive mindset really is: not just a catchy phrase, but a life-changing perspective.

- ➤ The mindset that quietly holds you back, often, without you even realizing it.

- ➤ Why mindset matters more than you think, especially in career reinvention.

- ➤ How to transform limiting beliefs into open doors, with practical, actionable steps you can start right away.

Before we begin, pause for a moment and ask yourself:

- ➤ What stories have I been telling myself that have kept me stuck?

- ➤ What if those stories aren't the truth, just beliefs I've carried around for too long?

Hang in with me, because the concepts here might challenge you, stretch you, and make you uncomfortable at first. That's a good sign. It means your mind is already opening.

When you feel a sentence hit home, **don't rush past it**. Stop. Reread it. Let it sink in.

Because this chapter isn't just something to read, it's something to experience.

And if you allow it, it can be the turning point in your journey.

Adopting an expansive mindset is the next decisive step, one that can open doors to possibilities you may not have dared to imagine yet.

Think of your mind as a room. When you have a **limiting mindset**, the door is closed, the space feels cramped, and the light barely gets in. Old stories and beliefs crowd the corners, telling you what you can't do, what you're not capable of, or who you shouldn't be.

An **expansive mindset**, on the other hand, throws those doors wide open. It invites light in and breathes fresh air into that space. Suddenly, the room feels bigger, possibilities become clearer, and you start to see opportunities you never noticed before.

> "The size of your thinking shapes the size of your future."
>
> – David J. Schwartz

It's in that openness that you begin to realize your limits were never as fixed as you thought; they were simply the edges of your current perspective.

In this chapter, I aim to help you open that door and step into a mindset that will support your growth, reinvention, and future. Ready? Let's dive in.

What Is an Expansive Mindset?

An **expansive mindset** is the belief that your abilities, skills, and potential are not fixed – they can grow, change, and evolve over time. It's the willingness to challenge the stories you've told yourself, even when those stories feel comfortable or familiar.

Having this mindset means you see challenges not as threats, but as chances to learn. It means you understand failure isn't the end, but feedback guiding your next move.

Henry Ford said this:

> *"Failure is simply the opportunity to begin again, this time more intelligently."*

An **expansive mindset** is about embracing curiosity, being open to new possibilities, and permitting yourself to become more than you ever imagined.

This mindset isn't just a feel-good idea; it's a practical, powerful tool that opens doors – doors to new careers, new roles, and new versions of yourself.

The Mindset That Holds You Back

> *"Man travels hundreds of miles to gaze at the broad expanse of the ocean. He looks in awe at the heavens above. He stares in wonderment at the fields, the mountains, the rivers and the streams. And then he passes himself by without a thought – God's most amazing creation."*
>
> – attributed to St. Augustine

If you're reading this, chances are you've felt it before: that quiet voice inside, whispering doubts about your potential.

Maybe it says, "Who are you to aim higher?" or "You're not ready for that now".

These are the voices of limiting beliefs; stories rooted in **fear**, **past experiences**, and **old programming** that keep you stuck in roles and mindsets that no longer serve you.

Sometimes, the most challenging part of changing careers or reinventing your life isn't the skills or the plan. It's the voice inside your head telling you:

- I'm too old to start over.
- I don't have the right experience.
- I'm not creative enough.
- What if I fail?

Can you relate to this? If yes, grab a notebook and **write down the one that feels most true to you** – yes, **actually write it**. We'll revisit it later.

Those are examples of limiting beliefs, deeply held thoughts that keep you stuck. They whisper doubts, plant fears, and shrink your vision of what's possible.

Limiting beliefs often feel so real because they frequently stem from genuine experiences or deep-seated cultural conditioning. For instance, your family might value stability over risk, and maybe you've faced criticism before when trying something new. Or you learned early on to "play it safe".

The tricky part is that these limiting beliefs often work unconsciously; you might not even realize they're shaping your decisions and quietly holding you back.

Please remember.

- They're not facts.
- They're just stories.
- And you have the power to rewrite them.

Read that again. Let it sit.

Why Your Mindset Matters More Than You Think in Career Reinvention

Your mindset is the **lens** through which you **view the world** and **yourself**. It shapes your confidence, your decisions, and ultimately the trajectory of your career and life.

In Chapter 1, we began by identifying the discomfort you feel; the restlessness that signals it's time for change. Now, it's time to confront the beliefs that might be quietly holding you back.

I trust I still have your full attention.

Many professionals are incredibly skilled yet feel trapped in unfulfilling roles. The missing piece isn't usually a lack of skill or opportunity: it's their **mindset**.

Psychologist Carol Dweck's groundbreaking research on **Growth** versus **Fixed mindsets** reveals how those who believe their abilities can grow are more likely to embrace challenges, learn from failures, and move forward with transformation. In contrast, a fixed mindset **keeps us stuck**, causing us to **fear change**, **avoid risks**, and **doubt our worth.**

A **Fixed mindset** is the quiet voice that says, "You either have it or you don't." With this belief, talent and intelligence are seen as fixed traits, leaving little or no room for growth. People who think this way often tend to avoid challenges, fearing that failure will expose their limitations, so they quit at the first sign of struggle. Instead of learning from others' successes, they view them as a threat.

A **Growth mindset** is the mindset that screams, "You can get better – no matter where you start." Have you ever seen someone who, no matter their setback, keeps learning, keeps trying, and somehow keeps getting better? That's the essence of a growth mindset.

From this perspective, abilities are not fixed; they can be built, sharpened, and expanded through effort, learning, and persistence. People with a growth mindset welcome challenge, see failure as a steppingstone, and draw inspiration from the achievements of others.

When it comes to career reinvention, a growth mindset is your key to the **next level**. It helps you to see challenges as opportunities, failures as feedback, and struggles as part of the journey, not the end of it. That is why you need to treat this chapter as your personal **mindset reset** a turning point where you start rewiring how you think, see yourself, and approach every opportunity ahead.

The Science Behind Expansive Mindsets

The excellent news science keeps revealing is this: your mind isn't stuck. It's flexible, adaptable, and ready to change, sometimes in ways that will surprise you.

Research in cognitive behavioural therapy (CBT) confirms that by deliberately shifting the way you think, you can reshape your thoughts, feelings, and actions. This isn't wishful thinking; it's a proven, repeatable process.

When you catch yourself in a negative thought loop and consciously choose a different, more empowering perspective, you're not just "thinking differently" – you're literally **rewiring your brain**.

This remarkable ability is called **neuroplasticity**, the brain's capacity to form new neural connections throughout life. Think of your mind as having a built-in upgrade system.

Those old, limiting beliefs? They're not concrete walls trapping you: they're more like curtains you can pull aside to reveal a whole new view.

I've seen this unfold countless times in the lives of my clients. One of them, a corporate manager, constantly heard an internal voice whisper, "Who are you to aim higher?"

Together, we uncovered limiting beliefs deeply rooted in her childhood experiences. Using **cognitive restructuring techniques**, she gradually transformed those doubts into empowering truths. Her confidence grew, her voice found strength, and she stepped into a senior leadership role that truly reflected her authentic self.

This is to show you that with the right mindset tools, you can dismantle the beliefs holding you back and build new mental pathways leading toward the life you've always wanted.

Cognitive Restructuring Techniques are methods used in psychology, especially in CBT, to help people identify, challenge, and change unhelpful or harmful thought patterns. The idea is to "restructure" the way you think about a situation so that your thoughts become more balanced, realistic, and positive.

For example, if you have a thought like "I'm not good enough to succeed," **cognitive restructuring** helps you to:

- Notice such a thought.
- Question its accuracy: is it really true?
- Replace it with a more helpful thought, like "I have skills and strengths that can help me grow and succeed."

It's basically training your brain to break free from limiting beliefs and develop healthier, more empowering ways of thinking. This technique is commonly used to **reduce anxiety**, **improve**

confidence, and **support personal growth**, like in career reinvention.

My Own Mindset Shift

If you recall my story from the introduction to this book, my journey of reinvention began with some of the exact mindset struggles you may be facing now.

Before I took one month off during my first pivot, doubt and fear were constant companions. I kept asking myself, "Am I throwing away everything I've worked so hard for?"

But then I realized something powerful: the identity that had defined me as a surgeon was also a box that limited who I could become.

Instead of seeing the pause as a failure, I began to view it as an opportunity to expand and explore who I might be beyond being a surgeon.

That mindset expansion made me who I am today.

Career reinvention to me wasn't just about changing careers; it was about growing into a fuller, more fulfilling self, without discarding who I was.

That shift allowed me to step into new roles with confidence.

From Limiting Beliefs to Open Doors

Think about the stories playing on repeat in your head. Maybe they sound like:

- ➢ I'm not qualified enough to switch careers.

- I don't have what it takes to be a leader.
- If I fail, everyone will judge me.

These stories don't come from thin air. They often trace back to moments in your past, a harsh comment from a teacher, a failed project, or even your own inner critic pushing you to "play it safe".

I recently supported a woman who described her struggle with haunting clarity:

She had great potential on the outside but felt like she was trapped inside a perspex box – visible to the world, but confined by invisible walls of doubt. In her words,

> *"I know I can do more, but something's holding me back – like I'm trapped inside a box."*

As we explored her thoughts, a few limiting beliefs emerged:

- I'm not good enough.
- I'm not capable of achieving much.
- If I try, I'll just fail again.

These beliefs aren't truths; they're old stories replayed over time, shaped by fear, past criticism by her spouse, and business setbacks.

Earlier, I asked you to write down your own limiting beliefs; those quiet but persistent thoughts that try to keep you small.

And as you go through this chapter, keep adding to the list if new thoughts surface, because sometimes the simple act of **naming your thoughts** is the first step toward **loosening their grip**.

If you're reading this and you hear the same voices or feel stuck inside your own invisible box, remember the discussion we had in Chapter 1: The first step is **awareness,** because you can't change what you don't notice.

From there, by being kind to yourself and embracing an expansive mindset, you can start to challenge those beliefs, break free from them, and open the door to new possibilities.

Remember, growth happens when you permit yourself to step beyond the walls that once held you back.

As you turn these pages, know that I'm right here walking with you every step of your Career Reinvention journey.

Before we dive in, go back to the list you wrote earlier regarding your limiting beliefs. Please email it to me now at david@davidonu.com. I will personally read every single one.

You've already taken the time to uncover what's been holding you back; don't let it just sit there. Sharing your limiting beliefs breaks that illusion and reminds you they're just thoughts, not your identity.

Breaking Free: Practical Steps to Shift to an Expansive Mindset

You've already spotted those stories that have been quietly holding you hostage. You can feel the invisible walls built by limiting beliefs closing in around you. Now, it's time to break free, but not by fighting harder or pushing through with frustration, but by intention and steady practice.

Breaking free isn't something that happens all at once. It's rewiring your thoughts and reshaping your life by taking deliberate steps.

And the journey begins with simple, powerful moves you can make right now to expand your mind and build unshakable confidence.

Please stay with me – this is where the fundamental shift begins. You might be wondering how. Let me walk you through the proven process, the same way I guide my clients, step by step, toward freedom.

These next steps aren't just ideas to think about; they're practical moves you can start using today to change how you think, feel, and show up in the world. This isn't some random advice; it's the real work that leads to breakthroughs.

1. Catch Your Limiting Beliefs Like a Detective on the Hunt

First, become the detective of your own mind. What stories are running your life from behind the scenes? Write them down clearly:

- I'm too old to start over.
- I'll never be good enough.
- If I fail, it's the end of the road.

These thoughts are sneaky. They creep in when you're tired, overwhelmed, or second-guessing yourself. But catching them in the act is your first power move. Awareness is like shining a flashlight into a dark room; once you see what's there, it loses its grip.

2. Smash Those Lies to Pieces

Now that you have gotten the limiting beliefs, don't just nod and move on. Grab the beliefs by the collar and challenge them hard.

Ask yourself:

- Where's the proof this is true?
- Have I really failed at everything? Or is this just one story I keep replaying over and over?
- What would I tell my best friend if they said this?

Imagine your mind like a cage built from lies, and the above questions are the sledgehammer. Use the sledgehammer to break the bars. You'll be surprised how quickly those "truths" crumble when you actually inspect them closely.

3. Write Your New Story – Loud and Clear

Here's where the magic starts. You don't just want to think positively. You want to believe in your new truths so fiercely that they drown out your old story and limiting beliefs.

Write down the truths that light a fire inside you:

- My skills are real, and I'm ready to grow.
- Failure is feedback, not dead-end.
- I'm worthy of big dreams.

Once you've written a few empowering truths, it helps to see how others have replaced their old beliefs with affirmations. Here are some examples:

- *Belief:* I'm not good enough
  Affirmation: I am more than enough and bring unique value to the world.

- *Belief:* I don't deserve success
  Affirmation: I deserve success and welcome it into my life.

- *Belief:* I always fail when I try something new
  Affirmation: Every new experience is an opportunity to learn and grow.

- *Belief:* I'm too old (or too young) to start
  Affirmation: It's never too early or too late to pursue my dreams.

- *Belief:* I'll never be able to change
  Affirmation: I am constantly growing and can change my life at any time.

Say the affirmations out loud. Write them on sticky notes, frame them on your wall, text them to yourself, record them as voice memos, do whatever it takes to own these new beliefs.

And remember: every time you replace a lie with a truth, you're not just rewriting a sentence – you're rewriting your story. Keep at it, and soon these new beliefs won't just be words; they'll be the way you live.

4. Take Bold, Tiny Steps That Scare You

Here's where most people fail: they think mindset change is just about changing one's thoughts. Nope. It's about doing. And it starts small.

- Send that message you've been putting off.

- Apply for that job that feels just out of reach.

- Say yes to the uncomfortable conversation.

Every single brave step rewires your brain. It proves to your mind, "I'm bigger than my fears."

5. Get a Coach or Mentor Who Will Hold the Mirror Up

I won't sugarcoat it; navigating this journey alone is **tough**.

When you're deep in the trenches, your mind throws all kinds of curveballs to keep you stuck. That's where the right coach or mentor steps in and makes all the difference.

- They see what you can't yet see.
- They ask the hard questions you're afraid to face.
- They provide you with the right resources at the right time.
- They keep you accountable and cheer you on, even for the small wins you might want to overlook.

Investing in coaching isn't a luxury; I've personally spent thousands of dollars in coaching to get me through my reinvention journey so far. In fact, coaching and mentoring are the smartest moves you can make. It's your secret weapon for fundamental, lasting transformation.

6. Be Your Own Best Friend – With a Little Extra Kindness

Change isn't a straight path. You're going to stumble and doubt yourself many times. When that happens, don't make it worse by being hard on yourself.

Treat yourself like you would a friend who's learning to walk again. Cheer on every wobble and every small win.

Growth can get messy, and that's totally normal. What really counts is showing up for yourself with patience and kindness.

Robin Sharma captures this perfectly:

> *"Change is hard at the beginning, messy in the middle, but gorgeous at the end."*

That means both personal and professional growth follow this same path. The struggle is part of the journey, but the destination is beautiful.

The Truth I Want You to Carry

Changing your mindset isn't about ignoring reality or pretending everything's fine. It's about choosing to believe in your potential and power to grow, even when the path feels uncertain and scary.

Your mind is your most powerful tool. When you learn to train it, you hold the key to a career – and a life – that fits you.

If you're ready to stop shrinking yourself and start expanding into who you're meant to be, this is your moment.

Summary

In this chapter, we explored how mindset shapes career reinvention. You learned that limiting beliefs – those quiet, persistent thoughts telling you "you're not ready" or "you can't" – keep you stuck, even when opportunities are within your reach.

We introduced the power of an expansive, growth-oriented mindset, where your abilities and potential aren't fixed but can grow with effort, curiosity, and deliberate action. You also discovered practical steps to start shifting your mindset from today.

The **key takeaway**: your mind is your most powerful tool. Expand it, train it, and you'll step confidently into the next chapter of your career.

In the next chapter (Chapter 3), we'll talk about defining your destination clearly and wisely.

But right now, while your thoughts are still fresh, hit "send".

Email the list of your limiting beliefs to david@davidonu.com.

I want to walk you through this, not just in words, but in action, because the journey is just starting!

ACTION EXERCISES TO START EXPANDING YOUR MINDSET

1. Write Down Your Limiting Beliefs
Spend five minutes journaling your biggest fears or doubts about your career reinvention. Be honest and detailed.

2. Question Them
For each belief, write down evidence against it and how you might see it differently.

3. Create Affirmations
Turn your challenges into positive statements. Example: "I am capable of learning new skills and succeeding."

4. Plan One Small Step
What's one small action you can take this week to challenge your comfort zone? Commit to it.

CHAPTER 3: DEFINE YOUR DESTINATION CLEARLY – KNOWING EXACTLY WHERE YOU'RE HEADED

"If you don't know where you're going, you'll end up someplace else."

– Yogi Berra

Before we dive in, let's play a quick game of imagination.

Picture this: you're packing for a trip. Your suitcase is ready, passport in hand, and you rush to the airport, buzzing with excitement.

But when you reach the check-in desk, the attendant smiles politely and asks, "Where are you flying to?"

And you say, "I'm not sure – just send me somewhere nice."

They'd probably look at you like you just asked for a ticket to nowhere.

"Somewhere nice" could be the Swiss Alps, a Moroccan market, or a Bali beach resort. But if you don't know which one, you risk packing all the wrong things or not even reaching your destination at all.

That's precisely what career reinvention feels like when your destination isn't clear. You might still end up "somewhere", but it's unlikely to be where you truly belong. Seldom will your energy, purpose, and joy all pull in the same direction, and this makes you spend more energy fixing mistakes than building the future you want.

In this chapter, I'm going to help you get crystal clear on where you're headed. We'll discuss powerful **self-discovery exercises**, **vision-shaping strategies**, and the exact **tools** you need in your Career Reinvention journey to find work that fits and a life that matters.

Dangers of Not Having a Clear Destination: The Problem with "I Just Want Something Better"

It's easy to say what you don't want. Most people are experts at listing what's wrong with their current situation:

- I don't want this job anymore.
- I don't want to feel stuck.
- I don't want to burn out again.

But when you flip the question and ask, "So, what do you actually want?" the answers often get confusing, vague, or even disappear altogether.

They might say:

- I just want to be happy.
- I just want to be my own boss.

- I just want freedom.

On the surface, these might sound like clear goals, but dig a little deeper, and they're open to endless interpretation.

What does happiness really mean to you? Is it:

- A job with a flexible schedule?
- More creative work?
- Less stress?

What kind of freedom are you chasing?

- Freedom to travel?
- Freedom to spend more quality time with your family?
- Freedom from a boss?
- Freedom to work on your own terms?
- Or something else entirely?

If you can't define what these big ideas mean for you, you're handing over the steering wheel of your life to chance, or worse, to other people's agendas.

Without clarity, you drift aimlessly. You might say "yes" to opportunities that don't align with your deeper goals. You might even follow trends that leave you more frustrated, not fulfilled.

Having a vague "I just want something better" mindset is like setting off on a journey without a map.

You might get somewhere different from what you hoped, or find yourself stuck in the same place, wondering why nothing's changed.

Clarity isn't **optional**: it's **essential**. It's the compass that guides you toward a career and life that truly align with who you are and what you value.

Why Clarity Matters

Clarity is like a **Global Positioning System (GPS)** – it only works when you input a destination.

In career reinvention, that destination serves as your guiding vision, shaping every decision you make.

Here's how **Clarity** works for you:

- It shapes your daily choices, helping you decide which roles to pursue and which to decline politely.

- It helps you trust the path ahead, even when every turn isn't visible yet.

- It protects you from drifting into jobs that feel "fine" but don't truly fit your purpose or values.

Take, for example, a mid-career executive I worked with. To an outside observer, he was a picture of professional success, with a respected title, a solid pay cheque, and a corner office. But inside, he struggled to imagine a life beyond that role; a life that felt meaningful and fulfilling.

Through **Guided Visualisation** exercises, he began to paint a vivid picture of his ideal future.

For him, it was the breakthrough he needed to confidently carve out a new path, one that aligned with his true desires.

Science backs this up. **Neuroscience** tells us that vividly imagining our goals activates the brain almost as if we were actually living them. This mental rehearsal helps strengthen your motivation and sharpens your clarity.

The Science Behind Clarity

Have you ever noticed how, once you decide to buy a particular car, you suddenly start seeing it everywhere?

It's not that every driver in your city bought the same car overnight.

It's your brain saying, "Oh, we care about this now – pay attention."

That's the power of Clarity at work.

Your brain is wired to filter the world through whatever you've told it matters most. In neuroscience, this is known as the **Reticular Activating System (RAS)**, which serves as your internal gatekeeper.

When you are specific about what you want, your RAS starts scanning the noise of daily life for anything that matches your criteria. It quietly pushes other things into the background.

It's the same reason elite athletes visualise the exact moment they win before stepping into the arena. They're not daydreaming. They're mentally programming their brain to recognise, prioritise, and act on anything that aligns with the picture they have in mind.

This isn't wishful thinking. It's **strategic mental training**.

The clearer your destination, the more easily your distractions fade, and the faster your actions line up to get you there.

Now that you understand how clarity works. Let me guide you through the proven, step-by-step **Career Reinvention Clarity Method**, making it easier for you to define your destination with clarity and confidence, rather than leaving it to chance.

Step-by-Step: Define Your Destination Using the Career Reinvention Clarity Method

Before we proceed with this section, please grab your notebook and pen. Go ahead and do that now.

Got them? Good.

Because what you write down in the next few minutes will become the **map** you keep checking when things get busy or uncertain. You'll want every moment of clarity captured on paper, not floating around in your head where it can fade.

You've got all the pieces: your skills, your ideas, your hopes, your experiences. But without seeing the big picture, you force pieces into the wrong places, you waste time, and you begin to wonder if it's even worth finishing.

Defining your career destination is how you turn daydreams into a direction you can actually follow. It's how you move from drifting to steering.

Without having a destination, you risk spending years climbing a ladder, only to find out it's leaning against the wrong wall.

The steps I will share are what you will come back to, over and over again, refining and adjusting as you grow.

So take your time. Be honest with yourself and don't rush the exercise. This isn't homework to finish; this is your life we're shaping.

When you're clear on your destination, you'll notice something shift.

- Decisions get easier.
- Obstacles feel smaller.
- You stop feeling like you're trying everything just to see what sticks, because now, you know exactly where you're headed.

I believe you are still with your notebook and pen. Yes, right? Good!

Now, let's go ahead to find out your destination – your personal compass for building a career and a life that truly fits you.

1. Define Your Big Why

Before you can chart your next career move, you need to know precisely why you're doing it. This "why" is your anchor, the reason you'll keep going when things get hard, and the filter you'll use to decide what's worth your time and energy.

Ask yourself, "What do I want my work to give me?" Is it:

- More impact?
- A higher income?
- Creative freedom?

➢ Better balance between work and life?

In Chapter 1, we discussed **Hygiene factors** and **Motivators**.

Hygiene factors are the basics that prevent dissatisfaction: things like fair pay, a safe work environment, reasonable company policies, good relationships with your boss, and job security.

Motivators are what truly light you up: achievement, recognition, meaningful work, and career growth. These factors satisfy your deeper needs for purpose and self-actualization.

Both matter when defining your why. If **Hygiene factors** are missing, you'll constantly feel stressed or resentful, no matter how inspiring the work is. If **Motivators** are missing, you might have a comfortable job, but you'll feel restless and unfulfilled.

Your "why" often lives at the intersection of where your essential needs are met and your deeper desires are satisfied.

Exercise: Find Your Seed of Clarity

Draw a simple Venn diagram with three overlapping circles:

➢ **What energizes you** – The activities that make you feel alive, creative, and engaged. Or your skills, passions, and Motivators.

➢ **What you value most** – The principles, ethics, and priorities you cannot compromise.

➢ **How you want your life to feel** – The lifestyle, rhythm, and balance you want your career to support.

Where these circles overlap in the middle, write what shows up again and again. That middle space is your **Seed of Clarity** – your compass for choosing work that fits who you are and how you want to live.

Exercise: Find your seed of clarity

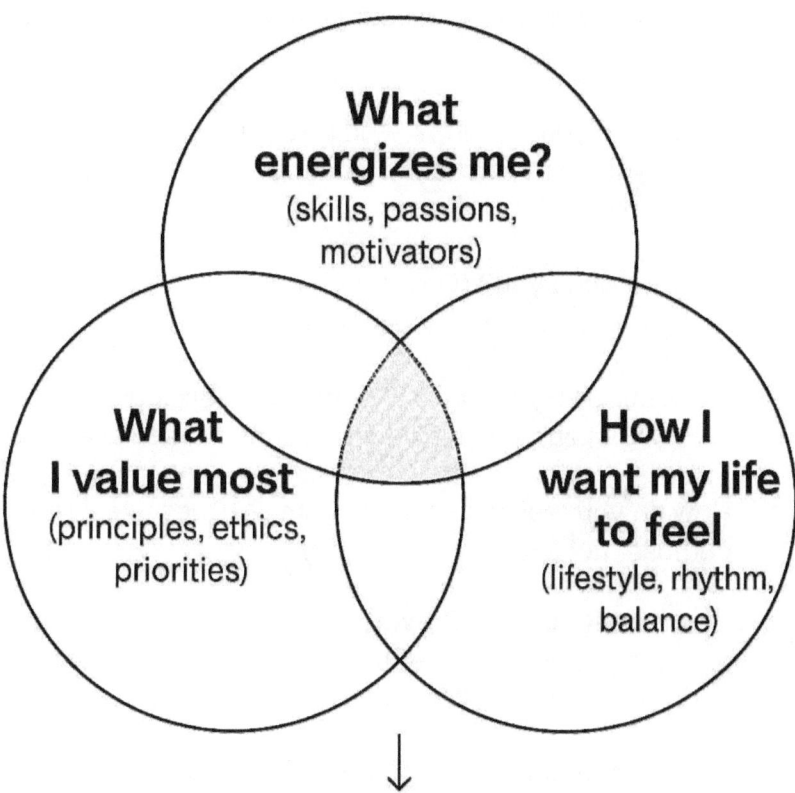

In the overlap of all three circles,
write what shows up again and again.

Seed of Clarity—

2. Paint the Picture in Detail

Settle into a quiet space. Picture your ideal workday ten years from now:

- Where are you working? (And does the environment meet your Hygiene factors: good working conditions, fair pay, stability?)

- Who's around you? (Do they support your Motivators: recognition, belonging, mentorship?)

- What tasks fill your day? (Are they challenging and meaningful enough to give you a sense of achievement?)

- How do you feel when you go home? (Does it feel like purpose, not just a pay cheque?)

Write it down as if you live it every day.

3. Set Your Non-negotiables

These are your boundaries. What matters enough that you'd walk away otherwise?

Maybe it's:

- No more working weekends.

- Not working under a micromanaging boss.

- I must stay aligned with social causes.

- I need flexible hours for my family.

These guardrails keep your career destination real and sustainable.

4. Test Your Vision With Reality

Now, check the path:

- Look for three to five people already living that vision and learn from their journey.

- Identify gaps – what skill, network, or mindset do you need to develop?

- Check market trends – ensure there's room for this vision to thrive.

5. Build Your Realignment Success Blueprint

Clarity without a plan is just a daydream. To turn your vision into reality, you need a personal blueprint (a living document) that pulls together what you've already created:

- **Purpose Statement** – Why this direction matters to you.

- **Vision Statement** – A vivid picture of your career and life.

- **Non-negotiables** – Boundaries that protect your wellbeing and values.

- **Skill Gaps** – What to learn next.

- **Possible Pathways** – Two or three routes to reach your destination.

Take a moment and look at what you've created – your big why, your detailed vision, your non-negotiables, and your blueprint.

These aren't just words on paper; they're the starting point of your future.

Think of them as your **personal compass**. It won't erase challenges or sudden turns, but it will ensure every step you take points toward the life that matters and the career that truly fits you.

Picture this: waking up to a day that feels right, making choices that feel natural, saying "yes" and "no" with confidence because you know exactly why they matter. That spark of excitement, that nervous thrill, that sense of possibility; that's your **North Star** shining through. That's **Clarity** finding a home inside you.

Keep your notebook close. Revisit it. Reflect and adjust.

Each time you do this, you're reinforcing the map of your path. Because what comes next, the moves you've been waiting to make, will feel lighter, more focused, and aligned.

Note: As you grow, your career destination may evolve, and that's part of the journey. Defining it clearly may require some research, and sometimes even exploring job listings, to identify roles that truly align with you. Do this after you've mapped out your personal compass using the **Career Reinvention Clarity Method**.

Confidence Boost: the Freedom of Clarity

When you have clarity, something shifts deep inside. Decisions that once paralysed you now land with confidence. You can now say "no" without guilt. You negotiate, act, and move forward, even when fear whispers "stop" – because you know exactly where you're heading.

Baroness Karen Brady said it best:

> "Knowing where you're going doesn't remove the obstacles, but it gives you a reason to keep walking."

Clarity doesn't erase challenges, but it changes the way you face them. Every obstacle becomes a signal, every setback becomes a step closer to the life that matters and work that truly fits you.

You're no longer guessing, stuck inside the invisible box. You're stepping out, intentionally, bravely, and with purpose.

Take a moment to breathe and feel that shift. That's the power of seeing your path clearly, and I'm right here with you, every step of the way.

(Optional) You Can Try This: Paint Your Future With Visualization

If you're still feeling stuck or unclear about your next step, here's a tool I've used with clients that has helped them change their career: **Guided Visualisation**.

Think of it as a mental rehearsal for the life you want. You're not just daydreaming, you're walking through your future as if it's already here, noticing the people, places, and work that make you feel alive. Your brain responds to these vivid images almost as if they were real experiences, quietly scanning for ways to make them happen.

Here's a quick Guided Visualisation you can try out in five minutes:

1. Find a quiet space – Turn off distractions and get comfortable.

2. Set your intention – One sentence about the life or role you want, e.g. "I'm thriving as a creative lead in a role I love."

3. Close your eyes and breathe – Slowly inhale and exhale to settle in.

4. Step into the future – Picture yourself three-to-five years from now in your ideal workday.

5. Engage your senses – What do you see, hear, smell, touch, and taste?

6. Anchor the feeling – Notice the emotions – pride, excitement, calm – and tell yourself, "This is possible."

7. Write it down – Jot down the details that felt most alive. Those are your career clues.

Do this a few times a week. The more clearly you can "see" your future, the easier it becomes to take steps toward it.

Summary

In this chapter, we explored why **defining your destination clearly** is the cornerstone of a successful career reinvention. Without Clarity, your career path is like booking a trip without knowing where you're going. You risk ending up somewhere that doesn't align with your values, purpose, or life.

We unpacked the dangers of vague goals, such as "I just want something better", and why they often lead to drifting into misaligned opportunities. Clarity, on the other hand, works like a GPS; it focuses your energy, guides your decisions, and filters out distractions.

Through neuroscience, we learned how the RAS helps your brain notice opportunities that align with your vision once you've defined it.

The heart of this chapter was the **Career Reinvention Clarity Method,** a step-by-step framework designed to help you map out your personal compass.

We also explored the power of guided visualization to rehearse your desired future and mentally strengthen your motivation. Your completed **Destination Blueprint** becomes your guide, giving you confidence to say "yes" and "no" with purpose and navigate challenges with resilience.

Now that you know exactly where you're headed, it's time to decide how you'll get there. In the next chapter (Chapter 4), we'll explore the two main paths of career reinvention – the **Quiet Pivot** and the **Bold Leap**. You'll discover how to choose the right approach for your goals, resources, and risk tolerance, ensuring your journey matches not just your destination, but also your **personal transition style**. The journey is just getting more interesting!

ACTION EXERCISE FOR THIS CHAPTER: YOUR DESTINATION BLUEPRINT

1. Write Your Purpose Statement

In one sentence, why are you reinventing your career?

2. Your Vision Statement

Describe your ideal work-life situation in vivid detail.

3. List Three to Five Non-negotiables

What you must stand for – and what you must refuse.

4. Skill Gap List

The skills you need to cultivate next.

5. Outline Two to Three Possible Career Pathways

Based on your vision and realities.

6. Set a Measurable Marker

A sign that you're on track (e.g. client number, course

completed, income goal).

Revisit this monthly as you grow.

CHAPTER 4:
SELECT YOUR PATH WISELY – DECIDE BETWEEN A QUIET PIVOT AND A BOLD LEAP

"It does not matter how slowly you go as long as you do not stop."

– Confucius.

Life rarely hands us clear, flashing signs when a decision matters most.

Sometimes, the choice arrives quietly, like a quiet fork in the road, inviting you to pause and sense which direction feels right.

Other times, it hits like a cliff in front of you, with nothing but a bridge daring you to leap.

One path is steady, measured, and predictable – a **Quiet Pivot** that lets you test the waters while holding onto stability.

The other? It's a **Bold Leap**: no guardrails, just a single decision that changes everything. Both can take you toward your next chapter, but the path you choose will shape the entire journey.

This chapter is about standing in that moment, where you get to select your path wisely.

In the last chapter, we explored how to define your destination, and I'm sure you've mapped it out and clarified your vision.

Now, the question shifts from "Where?" to "How?"

Do you make a **Quiet Pivot** that shifts your course bit by bit? Or do you take the **Bold Leap** that redefines your journey entirely?

This chapter will explore the difference between these two approaches. You'll know which one is right for the season you're in.

You already know life beyond your current career is possible and promising. But first, you must decide your **style of reinvention.**

When it comes to career reinvention, there's no one-size-fits-all path. It doesn't always mean handing in your resignation letter. Sometimes, it simply means expanding – stretching yourself into alignment with your true purpose. It means allowing your talents and skills to shine beyond your current job title.

Over time, these choices tend to fall into two main categories:

- The **Quiet Pivot**: a quiet, gradual shift that lets you keep one hand on the old while reaching for the new.

- The **Bold Leap**: a bold, rapid pivot that leaves no room for retreat.

Both can lead to a fulfilling next chapter, and both will stretch you in ways you didn't expect. The difference lies in how you move and how much risk and reinvention you're willing to take on at once.

I will break down both methods in detail for better understanding and informed decision-making.

The Quiet Pivot: Holding On Until You're Ready

I want you to picture this: You're stepping across stones in a rushing river. One foot stays planted firmly on the rock you know is steady, giving you balance and confidence. The other foot reaches forward, searching for the next stone. You pause, testing it to make sure it can hold your weight before moving. You don't rush; you move only when you're certain it's safe.

That's the **Quiet Pivot** – also called the **Trapeze Method** – in a nutshell: holding on to a role that is secure while carefully reaching for the next opportunity, moving forward only when you're ready.

It's when you keep one foot firmly planted in your current role while you quietly and strategically plan your next move in the background.

Scott Pape in *The Barefoot Investor* described the Trapeze Method as a strategy for transitioning from a secure job to a new venture without compromising your financial stability.

It involves **keeping your current job** while simultaneously **exploring your new idea** on a part-time or trial basis. Only when your venture shows promise, and you have a clear understanding of its potential would you consider leaving your job.

Here's a more detailed breakdown of how a **Quiet Pivot** really works:

➤ **Keep Your Safety Net**

Think of your current job as **the trapeze bar** you're holding onto. It helps you stay steady in paying your bills, avoiding debt, and giving you breathing space. Without it, leaping into something new can feel terrifying instead of exciting.

➤ Test Your New Idea

Here comes the fun part. You start **experimenting** with your new venture: a side hustle, a part-time business, or a skill you've been itching to try. Nights, weekends, and spare moments during your day become your practice time. You're moving forward, but still holding onto that bar, so you don't crash.

➤ Watch, Learn, Decide

For a while, say, around a year, you pay attention. How is it going? Is it sustainable? Does it feel right?

And when your new venture starts showing promise, you feel confident it could actually work, that's your signal: it's time to **let go of the bar** and **commit fully.**

General Applicability

This approach isn't only about jobs or businesses. Any significant life change, a move, a passion project, or even a lifestyle shift, can benefit from holding on a little longer while testing the waters. It's all about striking a balance between courage and caution – leaping while keeping yourself safe as you figure things out.

Here's how it plays out in real life:

- ➤ Taking evening or online classes to learn skills for your new career.
- ➤ Starting a side business on weekends while your 9-to-5 covers the bills.

- Volunteering or freelancing in your target field before you make it official.

- Observing or following someone who is already doing what you want to achieve so that you can learn from their actions, habits, and decisions.

Why people choose the **Quiet Pivot**:

- Most people have obligations – bills to pay, others to care for, commitments that won't wait.

- Sometimes, you're not ready to dive in headfirst; you want to test the waters first.

- Other times, the timing just isn't right for big, risky moves.

The **Quiet Pivot** lets you move forward carefully, holding on to what's steady while reaching for the next opportunity at your own pace.

The upside:

- Keeps your income flowing and your safety net secure.

- Gives you space to learn skills and experience at your own pace.

- Lets you correct your course if the new path isn't what you imagined.

The downside:

- Progress is slower.

- Balancing both worlds can drain your energy and push you toward burnout.

Sometimes, it's not about how fast you leap; it's about making sure the net is strong enough to catch you if you fall.

The Bold Leap: Letting Go to Move Forward

The **Bold Leap** is a different kind of story. It's that split-second moment when you let go of the job you've been holding onto, even before you've secured the next one.

- It's walking out of your 9-to-5 to launch the business you've been dreaming about, finally.

- It's moving into a completely different industry, leaving everything familiar behind.

- It's signing up for a full-time degree in a field you've never worked in, stepping into the unknown with nothing but courage and determination.

The **Bold Leap** is swift and intense.

Why do people choose the **Bold Leap**?

- When staying put feels unbearable, because the job is unbearable and suffocating.

- They have savings, investments, or a financial cushion to soften the landing.

- They thrive under pressure and want results immediately.

The upside:

- It builds massive momentum. You learn at lightning speed because you have no choice.

- This pivot method often sparks breakthroughs, resilience, and deep personal growth.

The downside:

- It's high stakes, both financially and emotionally.

- If things go wrong, the road to recovery can be longer and harder.

My Pivot Story

If you remember my story from the introduction section of this book, you'll know I've experienced both pivot methods.

In 2012, I made my first **Bold Leap**. I walked away from surgery – a profession I'd spent years training for, and a role deeply tied to my identity. It wasn't just leaving a job. It was stepping away from a respected title and the story I'd been telling myself since medical school.

At first, it was terrifying. And yes, it came with its fair share of financial, emotional, and practical challenges. But the growth and relief I experienced? It was faster and deeper than anything I could have imagined if I'd stayed.

Years later, I tried a different path – the **Quiet Pivot**. This time, I didn't jump; I stepped carefully. I began blogging, writing, coaching, and exploring thought leadership, all while continuing to practice medicine. I was building something new without letting go of what I already had.

And I realized something powerful through my pivots: you can **be successful** and still **feel restless**. You can tick every box on paper and still feel the urge to move forward.

But at the end of the day, the kind of pivot you make isn't really about being brave. It's about finding the move that fits **your situation**, **your personality**, and the **season of life** you're in. **(Read this twice.)**

Understanding these two approaches —holding on with the **Quiet Pivot** or making the **Bold Leap** – helped me see that career moves, much like leadership, aren't a straight line.

Stepping into a senior leadership role at the Tasmanian Health Service in 2022, I realized that building and leading a medical team mirrored the very same principles. That's when the **Employee Life Cycle** became my roadmap, both for my team and for my own career pivots.

The Employee Life Cycle

At the time, I thought I was just switching careers. But I soon realized that career moves aren't a straight ladder you climb step by step; they move in cycles.

And understanding where you are in the Employee Life Cycle can make all the difference. It helps you see your next move clearly, instead of stumbling in the dark.

I want to use my story to illustrate how I experienced each stage of the Employee Life Cycle and how it relates to pivoting your career.

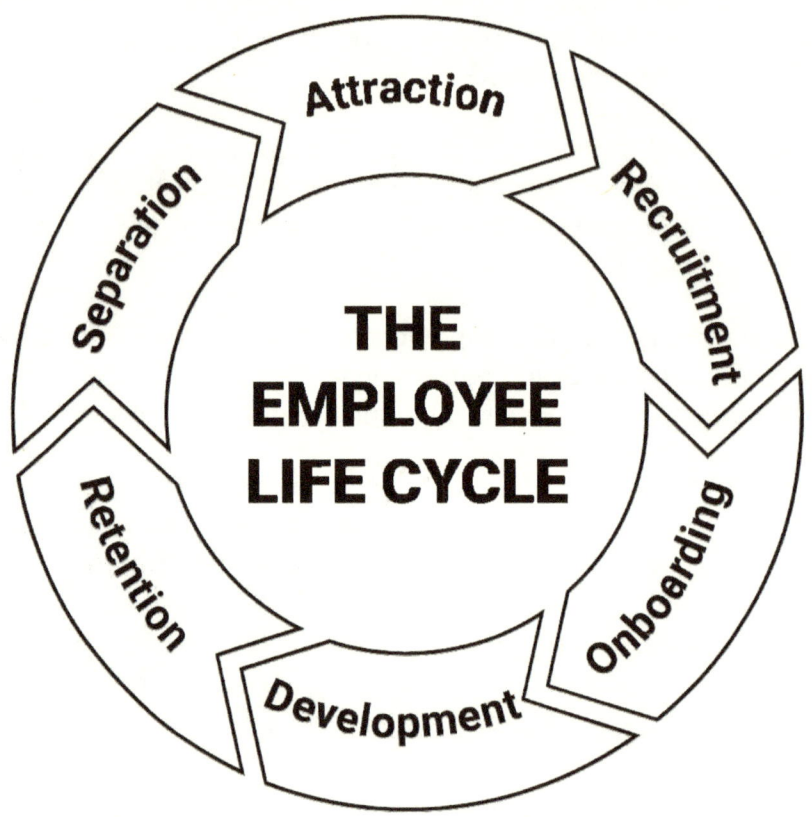

Here's how I navigated each stage and what it taught me about making strategic career pivots:

1. Attraction – This is where it all begins. I noticed an opportunity to build a strong medical team, and something inside me said, "I want to be part of that". Just like in your career, this stage is about curiosity and alignment with your values.

If you're here, the Quiet Pivot is ideal for exploring, testing the waters, and learning without burning bridges. For me, I spent time observing the chaos in staffing and imagining what a thriving team could look like.

2. Recruitment – At this stage, I had to position myself and the service to attract the right doctors. We leveraged professional networks, including LinkedIn, to offer locum-to-permanent bridges and highlight flexible work arrangements.

In a career pivot, this is your "planting seeds" stage where you network, sharpen skills, and make yourself visible.

3. Onboarding – Once new doctors signed their contracts, the real work began. The first days and weeks were about building trust, learning the facility's rhythms, and proving that we belonged together as a team. Because I've learned, if you want to make a strong team, you don't just recruit – you connect. I simply applied that, and I saw significant changes.

In your career, **onboarding** is **landing that new role** and **figuring out how to thrive**. Even a slight pivot requires this patience and intentionality.

4. Development – This is the **growth zone.** I led the team, provided mentorship, and discovered strengths in both me and the doctors I hadn't realized before.

In this phase, every win and every mistake taught us something new. In a career pivot, this is where you grow through **training, experimentation,** and **stretching yourself.**

5. Retention – Retaining talent is the actual test of leadership. In this stage, I realized that titles, systems, or strategy alone didn't keep people: connection, trust, psychological safety, and servant leadership did.

In your career, this is the moment to pause and ask: "Is this role or path still right for me?" Here, you weigh **progress**, **satisfaction**, and **long-term goals** to decide whether to stay or pivot further.

6. Separation – Eventually, every employee cycle reaches this stage. In leadership, it's about planning intentional exits without burning bridges. For career pivots, this is where the Bold Leap comes in as a clean, deliberate move into your next chapter when the timing is right.

Understanding the cycle changes everything. You stop guessing and start making thoughtful, strategic moves that get you closer to your career destination, whether you're leading a team or pivoting your own career.

For me, living through the Employee Life Cycle enabled me to recruit, nurture, and retain a team that transitioned from chaos to achieving "net-zero locum" status within 24 months.

And that's how transformation happens – quietly, powerfully, and humanely.

How to Choose the Right Pivot: Five Questions to Ask Yourself

At this point, you might be asking yourself, "So, which path should I take; the **Quiet Pivot** or the **Bold Leap**?"

Honestly, there's no magic formula for choosing the right option, and the method that works for someone else might not work for you. But asking yourself a few honest, and sometimes uncomfortable questions, can make your decision a lot clearer. Let's walk through them together.

Think of these questions as a self-check to help you figure out what really makes sense for you right now. I also want you to write down your answers to these questions in your notebook, as they will serve as a guide to help you choose the most suitable pivot method.

1. What's my financial reality?

Take a good look at your finances. Could you cover your living expenses for 6 to 12 months if no funds come in? Be honest with yourself, making a move while living pay cheque to pay cheque feels very different from making a move with a financial cushion to fall back on.

2. How do I handle uncertainty?

Some people thrive on the unknown. They view it as an adventure and an opportunity to embark on something challenging. Others lose sleep over it. Which type are you?

3. How urgent is this change?

Do you have the patience for a slow, steady transition, or do you feel like you've reached your limit and need a change immediately? Your timing matters.

4. Who's in my corner?

Do you have mentors, friends, or family cheering you on, helping you find opportunities, and reminding you why you started when things get tough? Having support can make a massive difference in the type of pivot method you choose.

5. What's my energy level?

I want you to be honest with yourself here. Can you realistically dedicate energy to something new while still managing all the tasks already on your plate? Or would trying to juggle both just leave you drained and running on fumes? Understanding your energy level is crucial when deciding which type of pivot is right for you.

Here's a quick cheat sheet to make things simpler:

- If your answers lean towards **security** and **caution,** the Quiet Pivot is probably your safest and most brilliant move.

- If your answers lean toward **change** and **speed,** the Bold Leap could be just the reset you need.

When choosing between the two pivot methods, I want you to remember there's no "better" choice. There's only the path that fits **you** and **your life** right now, and that's what you should consider.

By now, I'm sure you've gotten a solid grasp of the two pivot methods for career reinvention. And I hope you see that this journey isn't about rushing or copying someone else's path, but about making a choice that fits your life. Whether it's leaning toward the **Quiet Pivot** or the **Bold Leap**, what matters most is moving forward with **purpose**, **clarity**, and **a plan**.

Summary

In this chapter, we explored the two main ways to pivot in your career: the **Quiet Pivot** and the **Bold Leap**. You learned that the **Quiet Pivot** lets you hold onto stability while testing the waters for your next move. On the other hand, the **Bold Leap** is all about letting go and diving headfirst into the unknown, embracing change with intensity and courage.

We also examined the **Employee Life Cycle**, illustrating how understanding your current stage in the career journey can inform which pivot method suits you best.

Finally, we covered **five key questions** to help you make a choice that aligns with your financial reality, energy level, urgency, support system, and tolerance for uncertainty.

Now that you know the options, the risks and rewards of each path, and the approach that aligns with your life right now. The next step is just as important, building the right **Support Circle**.

That's why in the next chapter (Chapter 5), we'll dive into why reinvention thrives on connection and how having the right people around you can help you stay steady, motivated, and focused as you move forward. Later in the book (Chapter 8), we'll also explore Dr Ola van Steen's journey to see these ideas come alive in real life.

But before then, take a moment to breathe, reflect, and celebrate this milestone- choosing your path. Now, let's ensure you have the right people to lift you to reach new heights as you walk through it.

Reflective question for you:

> Which method are you leaning toward right now, and why?

CHAPTER 5: BUILD A SUPPORT CIRCLE – WHY REINVENTION THRIVES ON CONNECTION

"If you want to go fast, go alone. If you want to go far, go together."

– Burkina Faso proverb

In Chapter 4, we talked about choosing your path – whether you're taking a **Quiet Pivot** or making a **Bold Leap**.

By now, you've probably figured out which reinvention method fits you best. That's a big win, so take a moment to pat yourself on the back as we dive into Chapter 5.

I want you to know that choosing your path is just the beginning.

No matter how perfect your choice feels, trying to walk it alone will drain you faster than you think. It's like rowing across the ocean with just one paddle; you'll move, but not very far, and eventually, you'll be tired.

This is why building your **Support Circle** matters.

Reinvention thrives on connection. You need people who'll cheer you on, challenge you, and remind you why you started when doubt creeps in (and trust me, it will).

In this chapter, I'll be sharing more of my personal stories, not to impress you, but to highlight the great benefits of support networks along my own reinvention journey.

So let me ask you: Who's in your boat?

Read that again. Slowly.

Your support circle doesn't have to be hundreds of people; it just needs to be strong. These are the people who believe in your vision, even when you're still learning to believe in it yourself.

And let me say this: you don't have to wait for people to show up magically. Sometimes you'll have to intentionally seek them out by joining communities, reaching out to that person who inspires you, and starting meaningful conversations.

Having people around who can keep you steady when things get challenging makes the journey of building a new version of yourself a lot smoother.

So here's the question again: Who's in your boat, and are they helping you move forward or weighing you down?

Why Reinventing Without a Support Circle Sounds Good (But Isn't)

As you embark on your Career Reinvention journey, it's tempting to think, "I'll just figure things out on my own." It feels safer that way. No judgment. No raised eyebrows. No awkward explanations.

Sometimes it's not even fear of failure that prevents us from sharing our plans. It's the worry that people will assume we've lost the passion for what we're doing currently. So, we keep our plans close to our chests.

The problem is, when you try to handle everything alone, it's easy to lose perspective. Without encouragement, doubt grows louder. Without accountability, even your best ideas can quietly fade away.

Time and again, I've seen it: going solo on a reinvention journey often leads to burnout. But those with a strong support circle – mentors, friends, colleagues – move faster, smarter, and with more energy.

The truth is, no one climbs a mountain alone. You need people who **remind** you why you started, **nudge** you forward when you stall, and **celebrate** even the small wins. The right circle doesn't just make the journey easier; it makes the destination more meaningful.

My Support Circle Moment

Let me take you back to 2012, the year I walked away from surgery.

At the time, I had no idea how powerful a "support circle" could be in career reinvention. All I knew was that I had two people I could lean on: **my wife** and **a colleague**.

My wife was my anchor. She reminded me why I was making the change whenever fear whispered, "Go back." She believed in me even when I was unsure of myself, and that belief gave me the courage to keep moving forward.

My colleague, on the other hand, didn't just offer words of encouragement; he introduced me to a recruitment agency that opened the door to a role outside of surgery and the hospital.

That circle was small (just two people), but they made the difference between stalling and moving forward in my Career Reinvention journey. My wife's unwavering faith steadied me, and my colleague's practical help made the next step a lot easier.

It was still a profoundly personal and isolating time, as we had just relocated to Australia, and I didn't have a vast network of friends. But in that season, I discovered something important: you don't need a huge crowd to support your reinvention. Sometimes, just one or two people who believe in you and nudge you forward are enough to carry you through the most challenging transitions.

The Science Behind Support (Don't Skip This Part)

Let's pause for a moment.

I know you might be tempted to skip ahead to the "action steps", but trust me, this part is one of the most powerful pieces of your reinvention journey. Skipping it could slow you down more than you think.

Psychologists refer to the many benefits of our connections as **Social Capital**.

Sounds classy, right? But all it really means is this: the **resources** we draw from our **relationships**.

And when you're reinventing your career, that capital is worth more than gold.

Here's what it often looks like in real life:

- **Information** – A friend casually mentions an opening you'd never see on a job board. That one conversation could change everything.

- **Encouragement** – Someone looks you in the eye and reminds you, "You're more capable than you think." And suddenly, the doubts shrink.

- **Accountability** – A trusted voice asks, "Hey, did you send that application you said you would?" That nudge can be the difference between dreaming and actually taking action.

Now, I don't want you to just nod at this list and move on. **Reread it. Slowly this time.**

Because those three things – **information**, **encouragement**, and **accountability** – are the quiet forces that will carry you further than hard work alone.

I know this to be true because I've lived it.

In January 1992, I was preparing to enrol in Biological Sciences at the University of Calabar, Nigeria, as my first-choice course. However, a retired police inspector named Mr. Frank Ngwu then visited my eldest brother, who was my sponsor at the time. During that visit, he looked me straight in the eye and said, "David, you will not study Biological Sciences. You are going to study medicine. You have the brains to be a brilliant doctor – I believe in you!"

That single conversation shook me to the core. I took Mr Ngwu's words seriously, began the long process of switching to Medicine and Surgery at the University of Nigeria, Nsukka (my second choice), and seven years later, I graduated as a medical doctor. Looking back now, I realise that without that encouragement, my story might have been entirely different.

Years later, in 2008, another life-shaping yet straightforward moment occurred during my residency at the Ebonyi State Teaching Hospital in Nigeria.

One evening while on call, I crossed paths with two of my colleagues. In the middle of our casual conversation, they mentioned new opportunities to migrate to the Caribbean. That short exchange lit a spark in me. I acted on the information, and a few months later, my wife and I relocated to Trinidad and Tobago. Interestingly, those same colleagues also made the move.

These moments might appear as coincidences, but I view them as anchors and nudges. People showing up at the right time to encourage me, share information, or point me in a new direction. And that's what **Social Capital** really is: the quiet but powerful force of the right voices in your corner.

You can hustle all day long, but without the right voices around you, you'll lose the drive that keeps you moving forward. On the other hand, with the right social circle, even if it's just one or two people, you'll find yourself taking bolder steps, recovering faster from setbacks, and staying steady when fear whispers, "Go back".

I need you to remember something important here: you don't need hundreds of friends to reinvent your career. You don't need to be the most popular person in the room or have a long list of contacts in your phone. What you truly need are **the right people in your corner**.

As we delve deeper into this chapter, please pause and ask yourself: "Who are my anchors?" "Who are my nudges?"

Your **anchors** are the people who steady you when the waves get rough. Your anchors may include a friend, mentor, or partner who reminds you of your worth when self-doubt creeps in.

Your **nudges** are the gentle pushes that hold you accountable and keep you moving forward. The people who say, "Hey, didn't you say you were going to send that application?" or "Have you followed up on that idea yet?"

Both anchors and nudges matter. There may not be many, but they'll make all the difference whether you just dream about reinvention or actually live it.

Who Belongs in Your Circle

Like I mentioned earlier, you don't need hundreds of friends to move forward. You just need the right mix of people in your corner.

Think of your circle like a well-balanced diet served on a plate. If you overload on one food group, you miss out on the nourishment the others provide.

Here are the people you should have in your circle:

1. The Cheerleader: This is your **biggest fan**. They might not be familiar with all the ins and outs of your industry, but they know you. And when you forget what you're capable of, they'll be the first to remind you.

2. The Challenger: This is the friend (or colleague) who won't let you drift off into unrealistic dreams. They're the ones who throw the tough questions your way. The ones you'd rather dodge but secretly need if you're going to grow.

3. The Guide: This is the mentor, coach, or senior individual who's already walked the path you're on. They've stumbled, gotten back up, and learned the hard lessons. So you get to learn from them instead of repeating the same mistakes.

4. The Fellow Traveller: This is someone who's also on the journey of reinvention. You share the struggles, swap survival tips, and remind each other that the challenges are part of the process.

In my professional path as a senior doctor (and coach), I've written many examinations, which made my reinvention possible. At every stage of the journey, I made sure I wasn't walking alone. I always linked up with at least one colleague or built a small group of "fellow travellers" who acted as accountability partners. They made our journeys smoother and allowed me to do the same for others in return.

Take a moment and consider: Who came to mind for each role? Don't just think about it, write their names down. Because once you see them clearly, you'll be ready for what comes next.

How to Build Your Support Circle (Even If You Feel Like You Don't Know Anyone)

You may not have a support circle currently, and that's okay. Most people start small, or sometimes with no one at all. The good news? Circles grow over time, one person at a time. The key is to start where you are.

1. Look Around First

You might already know people who could be part of your circle, such as a colleague you trust, a friend who asks the right questions, or a former boss who believed in you when you didn't believe in yourself.

2. Join the Right Rooms

Be intentional about where you spend your time. It might be a professional or trade association, an online forum or platform, or even a local meetup. Basically, anywhere people like you are gathering. Sometimes, just one meaningful connection is all it takes to change your path.

3. Ask for Introductions

You may have to ask someone: "Do you know anyone who…?" People are usually happy to connect you with the right person. You simply need to be clear about the kind of person you're looking for and why. Also, don't be shy: introductions are how circles grow.

4. Start Small, Build Trust

You don't need to label someone as a "mentor" right away. Begin with a simple conversation, share your story, ask about theirs, and notice how the connection feels. The strongest relationships typically begin small, founded on honesty and consistency, and develop naturally over time.

Even if your circle is small right now or doesn't exist yet, taking these first steps matters. Never underestimate the power of a single conversation or connection. Together, they can change everything.

Next, we'll uncover the golden rule of support circles and how to keep the people who matter most by your side.

The Golden Rule of Support Circles: How to Nurture and Keep Them Thriving

A strong support circle isn't just about **what you get** – it's about **what you give**. How you show up, encourage others, and keep the people who matter close is what makes your circle truly powerful.

Celebrate others' wins, share your knowledge and resources, and be genuinely present.

Think of it like **planting seeds**: you may not see the fruit tomorrow, but one day, you'll look around and realize you're sitting under the shade of the very tree you helped grow.

We all know building a circle is important, but the real magic happens when you keep it alive.

Here's how to make that happen:

- ➢ **Check in regularly**: It doesn't have to be anything formal; a coffee, a quick call, or even a WhatsApp message works. Those little gestures go a long way in keeping connections strong.

- ➢ **Celebrate milestones**: Their wins matter just as much as yours. Cheer them on, celebrate their progress, and you'll see support come back to you.

- ➢ **Be honest about your struggles**: Vulnerability is magnetic. Sharing what you're going through invites deeper support and builds stronger, more genuine bonds.

A support circle only works when everyone shows up – not just for themselves, but for each other. Put in the effort, care for your people, and you'll be surprised at how your circle shows up for you in ways you don't expect.

Trim the Noise

Here's something everyone on a reinvention journey needs to hear: not every connection in your life is going to help you grow. Some advice is outdated, some people project their fears onto you, and some conversations leave you feeling drained instead of inspiring you.

That's why you need filters, especially now, when every decision counts.

Ask yourself:

- Does this advice align with my goals and values for my reinvention journey?

- Do I feel energized or drained after talking to this person?

- Am I seeking out enough perspectives so that one negative opinion doesn't knock me off course?

These are simple questions, but they're game changers. The stronger your filters, the healthier your circle, the sharper your focus, and the faster your reinvention journey moves forward. So, protect your energy, choose wisely, and watch your circle lift you higher than you ever imagined.

Remember: Reinvention isn't easy. Some days you'll feel unstoppable. Other days, you'll wonder what on earth you're doing.

That's precisely why your support circle matters. They won't undertake the journey for you, but they'll walk beside you, and that makes all the difference.

Surround yourself with people who believe in you, push you to reach new heights, and celebrate every step you take. Because with the right circle, reinvention stops feeling like a struggle and starts becoming a journey of real, unstoppable growth.

Summary

In this chapter, we explored why reinvention thrives on connection. You discovered how a strong support circle (**Cheerleaders**, **Challengers**, **Guides**, and **Fellow Travelers**) can lift you, challenge you, and keep you moving forward. We also discussed taking small, intentional steps, nurturing relationships, and reducing distractions so your energy remains focused on what truly matters.

In the next chapter (Chapter 6), we'll get honest about the invisible pressures that hold so many of us back. They include family expectations, cultural norms, and societal rules. We'll explore how to break free from them without guilt or regret. I'm sure you don't want to miss it, so read on and see what's waiting for you. See you there!

ACTION EXERCISE TO BUILD YOUR CIRCLE

1. Grab your notebook and write down who could fill each role: Cheerleader, Challenger, Guide, Fellow Traveler.

2. Be honest – where are the gaps? Who's missing? That's your next step.

3. Pick three people to reach out to this week. Message, call, or grab a coffee, just do it.

4. After each interaction, ask yourself: Did it lift you or drain you? Does it align with your reinvention goals?

5. Show up consistently. Small steps and intentional connections build a circle that genuinely supports your growth.

CHAPTER 6: NAVIGATE CULTURAL, SOCIETAL, AND FAMILY EXPECTATIONS – REINVENT WITHOUT GUILT OR REGRET

"Reinvention isn't betrayal. It's alignment, not obligation."

– Dr David Onu

Picture yourself at a crossroads, holding a map drawn long before you were even old enough to choose. On that map are paths carefully traced by family traditions, cultural expectations, and society's idea of a successful life – becoming a doctor, a lawyer, an engineer, or a manager – respectable titles, solid pay cheques, a life that makes sense to everyone else.

The problem? That map isn't yours. Every step can feel heavier than the last, like carrying a backpack full of everyone else's expectations.

Sometimes the loudest voices in your head aren't even yours. They belong to parents who sacrificed, communities that resist change, or a society that only applauds certain kinds of success.

And when those voices get louder, it's easy to start feeling guilty. The voice in your head says, "Am I being selfish? Ungrateful? Irresponsible? What if they're right and I'm wrong?"

This tug-of-war is familiar to anyone trying to reinvent themselves. On one side, **your culture and family**, the roots that shaped you. On the other hand, **your calling**, the life pulling you toward something different. And right in the middle? That's **you** trying to figure it out.

But reinvention doesn't have to be rebellion. You don't need to slam doors or cut ties to create the future you want. It's about alignment, not abandonment – honouring where you come from while daring to grow into who you're meant to be.

Of course, it isn't always easy. When your loved ones don't understand your choices, guilt can feel like a constant shadow. But remember this: you don't have to carry guilt as part of your reinvention. You can move forward with confidence and peace, without regret weighing you down.

This chapter is your toolkit for navigating one of reinvention's most formidable challenges: the people factor. You'll learn how to stay true to your path while navigating the voices, pressures, and expectations that surround you.

The Weight of Everyone Else's Expectations

Expectations rarely come empty-handed – they arrive dressed in love, culture, and identity. Families dream of safety, stability, and respect, nudging us toward secure careers and polished titles. Culture layers its own script, defining what feels honourable, while society turns up the volume, celebrating specific paths and quietly dismissing others.

When all of that collides with your own calling, freedom can feel like a burden. What should excite you becomes pressure. You spend more time trying to meet others' visions than listening to your own.

Reinvention demands **courage**. It asks you to separate your voice from the chorus, claiming what's truly yours and releasing what was handed to you.

This next section is your guide. We'll break down a six-step framework that keeps you on course whenever you feel pulled in the direction of someone else's path instead of yours.

The Six Steps to Reinvent Without Guilt or Regret

Reinvention doesn't mean erasing your roots or rejecting where you come from. It's about honouring your background while finding the courage to step into who you're becoming.

These six steps act as your compass, guiding you through **cultural**, **family**, and **societal expectations** toward choices that feel authentic, energizing, and true to you.

1. Awareness – Recognize the Voices Shaping You

Before you can reinvent yourself, you need to pause and pay attention to the influences around you. Expectations from people, traditions, or even unspoken rules can quietly shape your choices. If you're not careful, those voices can become so loud that your own gets lost.

That's why **awareness** is the first step. It's about asking yourself:

- Am I building a life that's truly mine, or one shaped by what others expect of me?

- Do my choices give me energy, or do they feel like obligations I can't escape?

- If nobody judged me, would I still choose this path?

Write your answers down. Seeing them on paper makes it harder to hide from the truth.

Think of it like loosening a tight knot. At first, it's tough to tell where one thread starts and another ends. But as you slowly work through it, separating your desires from their expectations, you'll begin to notice something: your own authentic voice. And that's the place where fundamental reinvention begins.

2. Clarity – Define Success on Your Own Terms

We're often handed a script about what success should look like: climb the career ladder, secure the big pay-check, earn the title. But that doesn't have to be your story, especially if you want more.

A six-figure salary sounds impressive, but if it keeps you stuck in traffic two hours a day and missing time with your family, is that really success? For some people, success is running a business from their laptop and being free to travel. For others, it's making an impact in their community, even if the income is smaller.

So pause and ask yourself:

- What kind of life feels good to me, not just on paper, but in reality?

- What matters more right now: security, freedom, impact, money, or growth?

> Ten years from today, what would make me genuinely proud, not just socially approved?

When you define success for yourself, the pressure to fit someone else's checklist fades. You're no longer trying to keep up with others' checklists; you're creating your own.

3. Communication – Talk With Respect, Not Rebellion

Conversations about your choices can feel heavy. Fighting rarely works. Express yourself calmly, explain your reasons, and show you value the other person's perspective. Understanding grows even if agreement doesn't.

Here's something I've learned: the way you say things often matters more than what you're actually saying.

For example, instead of blurting out, "I don't want to be a doctor," try framing it differently:

> *"I'm grateful for the opportunities my medical career has brought to my family, but I also feel my strengths and passions are leading me to pursue a path that allows me to explore my creativity."*

Notice the difference? It shifts the tone from **rejection** to **respect**. Rather than dropping your decision like a bombshell, walk them through your "why". Most resistance comes from not understanding. When you demonstrate that your choice still has room for growth, stability, or impact, it alleviates their concerns.

And don't just share the dream, share the plan. Uncertainty fuels worry, but a clear roadmap calms hearts and makes people more open to your journey.

This way, your loved ones can see your purpose without feeling rejected.

4. Integration – Keep What Fuels You, Release What Drains You

Reinvention doesn't mean leaving your roots behind. It's about keeping the parts that lift you and letting go of what no longer serves you. **Your** values, **your** lessons – they can travel with you as you move forward.

Think of it like getting ready for a long journey. You're packing a bag. Some things are essentials like discipline, resilience, and compassion. These are the tools that will help you thrive no matter where your path takes you.

Then there are the heavier items: rigid expectations, the pressure to chase a title, or society's never-ending checklist of success. Carrying those only slows you down.

The key? Hold on to what fuels you. Release what drains you. That's how you move forward intentionally.

Ask yourself these questions:

> - Which values have made me stronger and can still serve me in my future?
>
> - Which expectations feel outdated, limiting, or misaligned with who I'm becoming?

When you choose intentionally, you stop going through the motions. You're not tearing down your foundation; you're shaping it to be strong enough to support you and flexible enough to let you grow.

5. Boundaries – Protect Your Energy and Focus

Deciding to reinvent yourself is one thing. Living it daily is another. Even after you've taken bold steps, guilt and pressure can still creep in from others and even from within. That's why boundaries are essential: they don't isolate you; they safeguard your energy, focus, and growth.

Tips to practice boundaries:

- **Keep your "why" front and centre**: This is the anchor you identified back in Step 1 (Clarity). Write it down, visualize it daily, and revisit it when doubt whispers. Your "why" reminds you that the discomfort of boundaries is worth the bigger picture.

- **Limit draining conversations**: Think back to Step 3 when you practiced sharing your decisions. Boundaries take that a step further. You don't have to explain yourself or debate with everyone who disagrees with you. Sometimes, saying less and listening more is the most powerful move.

- **Surround yourself with the right people**: Focus on building a community that lifts you. Spend time with people who celebrate your growth and support your journey, rather than those who pull you back into old patterns or make you feel guilty for evolving.

Boundaries are like filters: they let in what nourishes you and keep out what drags you down. Firm boundaries help your reinvention stick, keeping you focused and confident.

6. Freedom – Accept That Not Everyone Will Approve

One of the most brutal truths about reinvention is that **not everyone will applaud you**. Some won't understand your choices. Some will criticise quietly. Others may distance themselves because your growth forces them to face their own fears.

But here's something I want you always to remember: you weren't created to live for universal approval. You were made for a purpose. Your mission isn't to meet everyone's expectations; it's to align with who you're becoming.

Even the most celebrated figures in history were misunderstood at some point in their lives. If they had waited for unanimous applause, they'd still be waiting. What carried them through wasn't approval but clarity of purpose and the courage to stay the course.

Absolute freedom comes when you stop explaining every move and let your results speak for themselves. Some doubters may go around over time; others won't – and that's perfectly okay. Their approval was never meant to be your fuel.

The real win is building a life that feels authentic in your own skin.

Keep these truths in mind:

- **Not everyone sees your vision**: Some are limited by fear, tradition, or expectation. That's their lens, not your burden.

- **Results speak louder than explanations**: You don't need to convince anyone, just keep showing up.

- **Approval is seasonal**: Opinions change when success becomes visible. But even if they don't, your fulfillment is not up for debate.

By following these six steps, you now have a roadmap to honour your roots while confidently stepping into your own path. You've got the tools to handle expectations, protect your energy, communicate with clarity, and embrace your freedom.

This is your guide to reinvention without guilt or compromise – your journey, on your terms.

So go ahead. Step into the life you've been imagining. The world doesn't need a perfect version of you; it requires the real you.

Summary

In this chapter, we explored how culture, family, and societal expectations can significantly influence your career decisions, and how you can navigate them without guilt or regret. You discovered why some pressures feel louder than your own voice, and how to distinguish what truly belongs to you from what belongs to others.

We also worked through a practical six-step framework to help you:

- Identify whose voices are shaping your choices.
- Define success on your own terms.
- Communicate your intentions respectfully.
- Integrate the values that uplift you while letting go of limiting expectations.
- Set boundaries that protect your energy.

> Accept that not everyone will approve, and that's perfectly okay.

These steps serve as your compass, guiding you with clarity, courage, and peace of mind as you reinvent yourself.

In the next chapter (Chapter 7), we'll explore a different challenge: the sacrifices people often make in the pursuit of ambition. Too often, success comes at the expense of your health, relationships, or happiness. We'll look at practical ways to achieve your goals without burning out, neglecting loved ones, or losing sight of what really matters.

You'll also learn how to create a life that balances achievement with wellbeing, making your reinvention sustainable and fulfilling. You won't want to miss it, so keep reading and get ready to take your reinvention to the next level.

Action Exercise for This Chapter

1. Whose Voice Is It?

- Write down three career beliefs you hold (e.g. "A stable job is the best path").
- Ask yourself: Did this come from my family, culture, society, or me?
- Circle the ones that are truly yours.

2. Define Success Your Way

Complete this:

"Success for me means ___, because it helps me ___ and makes me feel ___."

Keep it somewhere you'll see it every day, such as on your phone's wallpaper, your wall, or your desk, so it stays at the forefront of your mind.

3. Practice Your Boundaries

Write one short, respectful response you can use if someone questions your choice.

Example: "I appreciate your concern, but I've made this decision because it's right for me. Thank you for caring."

4. Keep What Serves You, Release What Doesn't

- List three family/cultural values you want to keep.
- List three expectations you no longer want to carry.
- Next to each one, write a small action you'll take to honour or release it.

CHAPTER 7: OVERCOME THE HIDDEN COST OF SUCCESS – PRIORITISE YOUR HEALTH, FAMILY, AND FULFILLMENT

"Success is not the key to happiness. Happiness is the key to success. If you love what you are doing, you will be successful."

– Albert Schweitzer

We live in a world that glorifies busy-ness. The fuller your calendar, the more successful you're assumed to be. That's the narrative we've been sold repeatedly.

Somewhere along the way, success got redefined. Suddenly, it became about job titles, bigger houses, and pay cheques with endless zeros.

However, no one discusses the fact that pursuing that version of success often comes at a **cost**. And you rarely notice it, until it hits you out of nowhere.

For some, the cost is a marriage that feels more like failure than intimacy. For others, it's kids who recognise your face but hardly your voice, or it's your body, breaking down from exhaustion.

My own awakening occurred quietly.

One evening, I arrived home and couldn't remember the drive. Nothing dramatic happened – no accidents or road rages.

But it was enough to make me realise that I had become a stranger in my own life. That's the hidden cost of success. It sneaks up quietly, while we're busy chasing more.

In this chapter, we'll uncover the hidden costs of success. More importantly, how to protect what truly matters – your health, family, and sense of fulfillment, while taking practical steps to build a life where success adds meaning, not emptiness.

Why This Step Matters (Especially as the Last Step)

The first six steps gave you the clarity, tools, and direction you need to aim higher and move smarter in your reinvention. But this seventh step? It's the one that keeps your reinvention alive.

Steps 1 to **3** helped you get clear and set your direction.

Steps 4 to **6** guided you through choosing your path and navigating people, culture, societal expectations, and more.

Now, **Step 7** is what ensures the life you're building can carry the weight of your success.

Without it, success can quietly drain you, leaving you exhausted instead of fulfilled. But with it, success doesn't just endure. It grows, it expands, and it feels complete alongside the people you hold dear. When you overcome the hidden costs of success by protecting your health, family, and fulfillment, you don't just win, you create a kind of success that truly lasts.

The Hidden Costs of Success

From the outside, success shines. But behind the gloss, many of us are paying prices we don't admit out loud. Below are the three most significant costs, so you can identify them early and protect what truly matters.

1. The Cost to Health

High-pressure roles require you to give your full energy every day. If you continue to give without refuelling, your body will send reminders: **headaches**, **restless nights**, and **constant fatigue**. Over time, real risks like **high blood pressure**, **anxiety**, or **burnout** may surface. You might tell yourself it's "just a season", but seasons have a way of stretching into years. You can't build lasting success on an empty body.

2. The Cost to Relationships

> *"I realize now that life is short, and we are very foolish if we do not keep a balance between work and family. If in trying to be a success, you lose your wife and family, you've lost it all."*
>
> *– Gary Chapman*

Success can quietly pull you away from the people who matter most. You miss dinners, break promises, or say, "I'll be there", only to cancel at the last minute. At first, your loved ones understand, but absence adds up.

Kids stop expecting you at their games, your partner carries the daily load alone, and friendships drift. Relationships rarely collapse in a dramatic moment; they fade quietly. Love speaks the language of attention, and you can't buy back the time you miss.

A decades-long Harvard study found that the happiest and healthiest people aren't necessarily the richest – they are the ones who invest in meaningful relationships. Achievements open doors, but relationships and connections make life worth walking through them.

3. The Emotional and Identity Cost

When you define yourself only by what you achieve, every milestone becomes a moving target. You hit a goal and feel strangely flat.

Your dream promotion or long-awaited accomplishment can leave you asking, "Is this all there is?"

Achievements matter, but without grounding in purpose, values, and meaningful connections, even success can feel hollow.

Practical Steps to Overcome the Hidden Costs of Success

Recognising the hidden costs of success is essential, but identifying them isn't enough if you don't take steps to protect what matters most. All the achievements in the world won't make up for what you've lost along the way.

This is where action comes in. These practical steps are meant to help you take care of your health, nurture your relationships, and preserve your sense of fulfillment, so your success doesn't come at a high cost:

1. Conduct a Life Audit

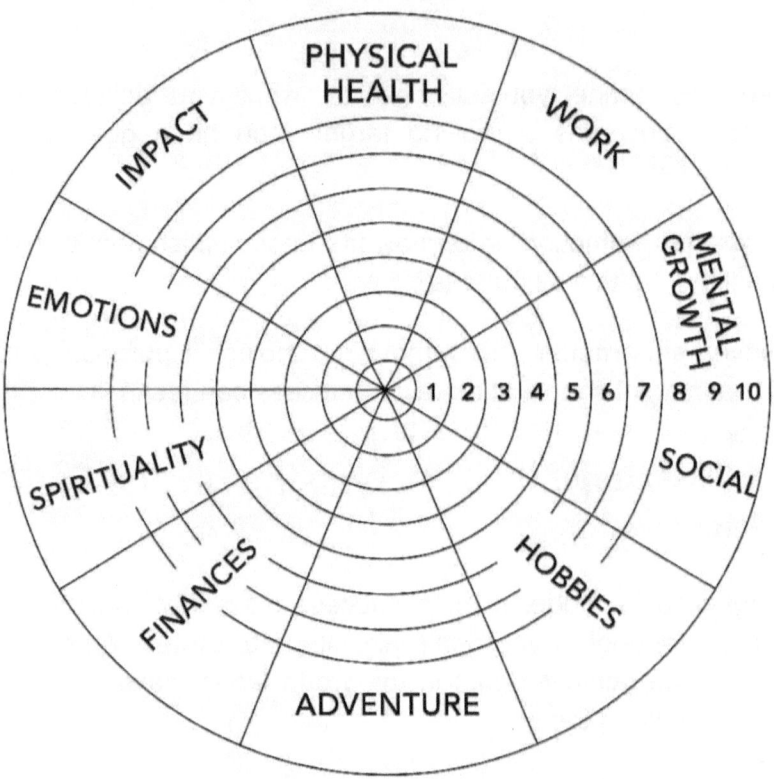

Imagine your life as a wheel with ten spokes, each representing a key area of your life.

Take a moment to rate each area on a scale of 1 to 10, based on the attention and energy you are currently giving it.

A score of 10 means this area is thriving and fully nourished, while **a score of 1** means it's neglected and needs urgent attention. The goal isn't to have a perfect 10 in every spoke, but to identify areas that are out of balance or areas for improvement.

- **Physical Health** – Your overall wellbeing, fitness, rest, and energy levels.

- **Work** – Career, business, or professional pursuits, and the satisfaction you get from them.

- **Mental Growth** – Learning, personal development, and expanding your knowledge and mindset.

- **Social** – Friendships, connections, and the quality of your social life.

- **Hobbies** – Activities you enjoy simply for fun, creativity, or relaxation.

- **Adventure** – Travel, new experiences, and stepping outside your comfort zone.

- **Finances** – Money management, income stability, and your sense of financial security.

- **Spirituality** – Faith, inner peace, values, and connection to something greater than yourself.

- **Emotions** – Emotional health, resilience, and how you manage stress or joy in daily life.

- **Impact** – The difference you make in the world, through contribution, service, or legacy.

Most of us pour energy into work or productivity, leaving other spokes – like health, relationships, or personal growth – thin and fragile. Once you've scored your wheel, you'll see which areas need more attention. From there, you can make intentional shifts to bring greater balance, so your life moves forward smoothly, rather than wobbling on a lopsided wheel.

2. Set Non-negotiable Boundaries

Choose one boundary you won't compromise. No emails after 8pm? A strict Sunday family day? Delegate tasks when you can and focus your energy on the habits that actually move you forward. Boundaries are essential for sustaining both your success and your wellbeing.

3. Reconnect With Loved Ones

Bring back the **little rituals** that keep relationships strong: family dinners, bedtime stories, weekly calls, or regular date nights. These moments aren't just nice to have; they're the glue that makes life meaningful.

4. Prioritise Health Daily

Small, consistent steps can make a big difference: twenty-minute walks, drinking more water, going to bed a bit earlier, or taking quick stretches at your work desk. Caring for your body isn't just a luxury; it's an investment in your future.

5. Create a Fulfillment List

Write down the hobbies, passions, and small activities that genuinely bring you joy. Then commit to taking one small step each week and actually follow through with it. Success should leave room for the things that make you feel alive, not just for what looks impressive on paper.

6. Listen to Your Body

Pay attention to the signals: stiff neck, headaches, low back pain, sleepless nights. Don't wait for them to turn into serious alarms.

Studies consistently show that prolonged stress from high-pressure roles can increase the risk of chronic illnesses, mental health challenges, and strained relationships. Paying attention early can save you from much bigger problems down the line.

Take Robert's story, for example. He's a successful entrepreneur, but despite his achievements, he told me he felt empty and disconnected from his family. When we looked closer, it became clear: work was taking priority over the moments that truly mattered.

During our sessions, I shared the exact practical steps outlined above with him, and he implemented them. The result was transformative. He didn't need one dramatic gesture; just the steady consistency of these non-negotiables made all the difference.

Today, Robert leads a balanced, purposeful life. His story demonstrates that by following these steps, you can overcome the hidden costs of success. You will protect your health, nurture your relationships, and create a life that feels balanced and truly fulfilling, not just accomplished.

Reflection

When the applause fades and the spotlight move on, what's really left? Not the titles, not the money, not the awards. It's the little things, like the laughter around the table, the energy in your body, and the quiet moments of peace, that stick with you.

So ask yourself these questions:

- What hidden costs are my version of success incurring?
- Am I giving up my health, my family, or my joy just to keep "winning"?
- If I keep living like this for five more years, what will it cost me?

These aren't easy questions, but they're precisely what you need to ask.

Success should energise you, not drain you. And that only happens when achievement lives alongside wellbeing. When ambition dances with joy, and when victories never come at the expense of the people and health that matter most.

Don't wait for a **health scare**, a **family crisis**, or an empty **victory lap** to force you to pause.

Take a breath now. Remember, these questions aren't here to shame you; they're here to help you. Because reinvention isn't about fixing what's broken, it's about creating what's possible.

Summary

In this chapter, we explored the hidden costs of success: how chasing career and financial goals without care for your health, relationships, and emotional wellbeing can leave you feeling empty. You discovered how to conduct a life audit, set boundaries, reconnect with loved ones, prioritise health, and make space for fulfillment.

As the final step in this Career Reinvention Blueprint, Chapter 7 reminds you that success is not just what you achieve, it's what you preserve: your **health**, your **relationships**, and your **peace of mind**.

A Quick Recap of the 7 Steps

Now that you've worked your way through the full Career Reinvention Blueprint™, let's take a moment to look back at everything you've explored and see how far you've already come.

1. Identify Your True Discomfort: Be honest with yourself: Are you just tired, or are you truly ready for change?

2. Adopt an Expansive Mindset: Break free from the limiting beliefs that have been holding you back.

3. Define Your Destination Clearly: Know exactly where you're going and why it matters.

4. Select Your Path Wisely: Decide whether your next move calls for a Quiet Pivot or a Bold Leap.

5. Build a Support Circle: Surround yourself with people who lift, guide, and encourage you.

6. Navigate Cultural and Family Expectations: Move forward without guilt, regret, or compromise of your values.

7. Overcome the Hidden Cost of Success: Protect your health, relationships, and overall fulfillment.

By now, you've likely started putting these steps into action. You've named your actual discomfort, expanded your mindset, and clarified your destination. You've chosen your path with intention, built a circle of support, honoured family and cultural expectations, and begun protecting your health and relationships from the hidden costs of success.

These seven steps aren't just a roadmap: they're a living blueprint. And if you've been applying what you've learned so far, I'm confident you'll see real, tangible results in your Career Reinvention journey.

THE 7 STEPS OF CAREER REINVENTION

To transition from where you are to where you want to be, follow these 7 proven steps:

IDENTIFY YOUR TRUE DISCOMFORT
Get honest about whether you're just tired or truly ready for change.

ADOPT AN EXPANSIVE MINDSET
Break free from the limiting beliefs holding you back.

SELECT YOUR DESTINATION CLEARLY
Know exactly where you're headed and why.

SELECT YOUR PATH WISELY
Decide whether you need a quiet pivot or a bold leap

BUILD A SUPPORT CIRCLE
Surround yourself with people who lft, guide, and encourage you.

NAVIGATE CULTURAL AND FAMILY EXPECTATIONS
Move forward without guilt or regret.

OVERCOME THE HIDDEN COST OF SUCCESS
Protect your health, relationships, and fulfillment.

THE CAREER REINVENTION BLUEPRINT™

In the next chapter (Chapter 8), you'll see these steps come to life through the remarkable story of Dr Ola van Steen. She faced challenges, made bold moves, and navigated her career reinvention with strategy and courage, emerging stronger, wiser, and entirely in charge of her life. Her journey will inspire you and prove that career reinvention is truly possible when you take intentional, fearless action.

Read on!

PART 2

THE STORIES – REAL JOURNEYS OF REINVENTION

Real stories remind us that reinvention isn't reserved for the fearless – it's written by those who had the courage to begin, afraid.

CHAPTER 8: FROM INTENSIVE CARE TO FREEDOM – DR OLA VAN STEEN'S JOURNEY

Trigger Warning

This chapter contains descriptions of war, loss, bullying, and emotional challenges. If you feel distressed, please pause and seek support from a trusted health professional or helpline.

> *"Your time is limited, so don't waste it living someone else's life."*
>
> – Steve Jobs

Up to this point, you've explored the complete Career Reinvention Blueprint: seven practical, life-changing steps to help you shift from where you are to where you're meant to be. But principles and steps only come alive when we see them in real lives, in real moments of choice.

That's what this chapter is about.

Here, you'll walk through the remarkable reinvention journey of **Dr Ola van Steen** – a woman who checked every box of traditional success, yet found herself longing for freedom, creativity, and a life that truly aligned with her purpose.

Her story shows both the challenges and breakthroughs that come with reinvention: navigating expectations, battling burnout, choosing courage, and finally discovering fulfillment on her own terms.

As you read, notice how each stage of her story connects back to the seven steps you've just completed. This isn't just a story; it's proof that reinvention is possible, even when the odds seem stacked against you.

The Influence Which Led Me to Study Medicine

I never really wanted to study medicine, so my story of reinvention started right after high school.

Though I had the grades that would get me into medical school, what I really wanted was to be a dentist.

Studying medicine was my mother's dream, and for a long time, it remained unfulfilled due to family and cultural reasons. So, when my grades screamed "this is possible", she had me live it for her. There really wasn't another option.

Still, there was always this little voice in my mind whispering: "This isn't what you wanted. This isn't the end."

However, I entered the medical field, and I performed very well. Really well. Outstanding marks, solid performance – all of it.

Graduation in the Aftermath of War

I graduated from medical school in 2007, right in the thick of the war in Iraq. Things were escalating so quickly that my family and I had to escape in a rush.

We migrated to Dubai – a city that, for so many, represents dreams, opportunities, and new beginnings. But for me, at that moment, it felt nothing like that.

I felt lost: I had no network, no proper paperwork, and absolutely no idea what to do with myself. A question kept ringing in my head: "Do I reinvent my career entirely or continue in medicine?"

It wasn't an easy choice. After six years in medical school, the thought of starting over from scratch, sitting in classrooms again, or switching careers altogether felt overwhelming. I simply couldn't stomach it.

So, standing at that crossroads, I chose the path of least resistance. I decided to continue in the medical field and started searching for jobs.

Early Career Survival

From 2008 to 2009, I worked as an unpaid intern in Dubai. It wasn't glamorous, but it was invaluable. I also learned a great deal about myself, including my resilience, my limits, and my drive.

But survival wasn't enough. I wanted growth. To grow, I had to step into the unknown again, this time by moving to another country in search of a paid job.

It took three exams and three interviews before I finally secured a training position in Internal Medicine at the American University of Beirut in Lebanon. Residency there was gruelling: 100-hour weeks, endless night shifts, and constant pressure. Yet, in between, I studied for the Royal College of Physicians membership exams, because I knew every step mattered.

When the time came, I had three tempting job offers to stay in Beirut and pursue fellowship training. But a quiet restlessness had taken root. I had outgrown the place. I wanted stability. I tried to unlock my full potential. And deep down, I was still searching for a country I could truly call home after being displaced by the war.

So, I leaped.

I sent out fifty-two applications. Fifty came back as rejections. Only two turned into offers.

So, in August 2012, I accepted a training position in Intensive Care medicine in the UK.

But my hunger didn't stop there. A year later, I decided to expand my scope, applying to dual train in acute medicine as well, because I knew my career wasn't just about surviving anymore. It was about building a life of impact.

The Internal Battle and Restlessness

I had all the qualities – I still do – that would make me an excellent and competent doctor. Yet internally, I lived with a constant battle: this is not me.

This is not my purpose. I did a fantastic job, but doing the job didn't make me feel great.

A quiet voice whispered inside me, reminding me that there's another life I'm meant to be living. The vision grew more vivid with each passing day.

But how do I get there? That's what I always wondered.

One day, I caught myself saying to a colleague, "I want to do something that makes my soul sing." I paused and realised the void I had within my soul ever since I stopped singing for years. There was a sense of relief because I could finally fill that void.

But naming it brought a new challenge: how could I make my soul sing again?

The longer I stayed without answers, the more I felt I was betraying myself. Yet leaving felt like betraying the profession I had poured years into.

Still, deep down, I knew this wasn't the end.

There was more for me: more impact, more growth, more contribution.

It felt like I had a treasure chest hidden somewhere, but I just hadn't found the key. And every time I hit a glass ceiling, it made me rebel harder against the life I was "supposed" to accept.

When people ask me, "Why did you leave medicine?" There's never a straight answer. It was both push and pull factors: the call of something greater, and the weight of something I could no longer carry, that led me to leave medicine behind eventually.

Consultant Years and Burnout

When I took my consultant job in 2019, the parts of the job I loved most were teaching, training, and education. However, that space was already occupied by more senior consultants. Instead, I ended up taking on a role in research, a role that crushed my soul and deepened my resentment and yearning to do something that actually fulfilled me.

The job's growing demands left little space for my creative outlets: reading, writing, travelling, exploring new places, and gathering new experiences. All the things that nourished me were slipping away.

And so, the rift within me grew wider.

I began asking uncomfortable questions:

- What else is out there?

- What do I need to do differently to create the change I crave?

- What does accurate alignment look like –the kind that fills my cup, rather than draining it?

Discovering My Destination

I navigated through a lot of options before, through quite an interesting turn of events, I came across an opportunity to set up a travel business. I decided to take it up in April 2020.

It was something I loved: travel, creativity, and freedom. A fully flexible business model where I wasn't confined in a box and there was no glass ceiling. I could shape it however I wanted. This offered a contrast to medicine, where everything is governed by rules, regulations, guidelines, and protocols, and where I had always felt trapped, with no space for creativity.

The travel business felt like the complete opposite. I could work from anywhere, follow my curiosity, and the risk was low enough that I could dive in quickly. My worst-case scenario was staying in the job I already had. I was living that worst-case scenario, and it pushed me to make the business work.

For the first time in years, I let my childlike curiosity come alive and play. In medicine, that part of you gets locked away because it doesn't fit inside the rules and protocols. In business, I could explore. I could make mistakes, and instead of being punished for them, I learned from them. Each mistake made me better.

It was like finding an oasis in the middle of a desert. Suddenly, I could breathe again. I could be the creative person I had buried for years. I started reading, writing, traveling, creating new experiences, and mentoring others. I was back to doing the things I loved most, the very things I had missed so much in my job.

It ticked all the right boxes for me. And slowly, my soul started to sing again!

Colleagues' Reactions and Toxic Pushback

As I was finding joy again, my work colleagues started noticing the business I was building on the side. Some treated it like a mistress I should be ashamed of.

Starting a travel business in the middle of a global pandemic raised eyebrows, of course. Stress and anxiety were already running high. Whether their reaction was out of fear for me – fear that I had lost the plot – or even jealousy that I had found something that made me happy, I'm not sure.

What I do know is that their resentment grew. The feeling among some was that if I had extra time, I should spend it working more shifts. The toxicity started to rise. The "boys' club" that I hadn't felt part of became even more difficult to access. Have you ever been in a conversation but not really part of it? That's how it felt.

Instead of being swept up in that tide, I poured my energy into my new business. I was learning, evolving, and growing. And the more I grew, the less the toxicity mattered.

By 2021, I pushed to reduce my work hours, but my managers refused. I wasn't trying to leave medical practice at that point; I was simply searching for a happy middle ground, the so-called work-life balance.

Both of my managers, two men, were against me: paternalistic and dismissive, telling me what was best for me while showing little acknowledgment that I could make my own choices.

I ended our conversation by resigning from my consultant role in acute medicine. I kept my sessions in Intensive Care but worked part-time. That choice gave me space – space for my vision, my purpose, and myself.

The Breaking Point

The occupational hazards of my job caught up with me. I suffered from Covid, then post-Covid fatigue, and eventually burnout.

The only bright side was that my business gave me breathing room to step away, even if only a little.

During that time, I met my husband while travelling. As countries slowly reopened their borders, we continued to date across the world. My soul was now singing in full force. We got engaged in 2022 and started planning our wedding for the following year.

However, when I reviewed the work roster, I realised there was no way I could take the time I needed to celebrate and create a new life together. The pandemic had already been a wake-up call – a stern reminder of who and what truly matter in life, and how often our time doesn't align with our values.

For me, the balance was completely off. I was giving my best years to a job that drained me, surrounded by people who struggled to be happy for me, who couldn't even offer a kind word. At the same time, I was being denied the space to grieve properly. I lost my grandmother to cancer during the pandemic, and because of lockdowns and work restrictions, I couldn't travel to see her. That pain stayed with me.

All of this forced me to reflect: "What choices do I need to make today so I don't keep living in this cycle, again and again?"

The answers weren't coming from work. Very few colleagues celebrated my choices. Some quietly said I was brave, even admitting they wished they could do the same. Others were indifferent. And some, as always, held onto their resentment.

Before I completely resigned from Intensive Care, I tried to find a way through. I worked with a life coach and even spoke with one of the hospital's career development coaches. The latter suggested I take a career break or a sabbatical.

But when I informed my manager, it wasn't even a consideration. Just a flat, "not possible".

I tried to negotiate reducing my work hours, but the only version they would accept meant keeping the out-of-hours on-call schedule, while cutting daytime sessions. It wasn't a sustainable combination: not from a physical, mental wellbeing, or clinical skills perspective.

No option for fewer hours. No option for a break. No option for balance.

That left me with the only option I didn't want to face: resigning completely.

On a logical level, it made perfect sense. But bringing that decision from my mind onto paper was the most challenging part, even though I had already resigned in my heart long before I put it in writing.

Support Network

During this period of transition and transformation, my support network was small but incredibly powerful.

My husband was my anchor. He believed in me so profoundly, constantly reminding me of my strength and resilience when I doubted myself. Trust me, the moments of doubt came more often than I liked, but he was always there, reminding me of what I'm capable of.

Alongside him, my business mentors and the thought leaders I followed through their books and podcasts became guiding lights, offering perspective, wisdom, and encouragement even from afar.

And then there were the people who believed in me enough to start working with me. They saw the vision and became part of my network, showing me that I wasn't navigating this reinvention alone.

Their faith, guidance, and presence gave me the courage to keep moving forward, even when the path felt uncertain.

Resignation Trigger

One weekend, I was on call in the Intensive Care unit. I stepped out of the office to gather the junior doctors for a ward round when I noticed one of them standing there, looking shaken, fighting back tears.

He had just received the news that his mother had passed away. For the past three months, he'd been trying to get permission to see her, but was unable to do so.

I told him to go home with his friend.

Then I walked back into the office, sank into my chair, and began to cry.

I didn't want that to be me, the one who gets that phone call at work, hearing those words, feeling the guilt rise as they have not been able to keep work at bay and spend more time with their family.

As I sat there, my manager walked in. Tears were still running down my face when he looked at me and asked, in a tone that wasn't really a question but more of an instruction: "Are you going to do the brainstem testing on bed 20?"

I looked at him in disbelief. Not because I planned on neglecting my work – I knew I'd get it done. But there was not even a flicker of compassion.

I wiped my tears and said, "Yes, it's on my list. A junior doctor needed to go home; he just lost his mum. I'm giving everyone some time to regroup, and then we'll finish the ward round."

He nodded, acknowledging the news, and then simply said he was off duty and headed home.

I turned back to my computer. Opened the draft resignation letter that had been sitting there for weeks. And I signed it.

I finished the ward round and stayed on-call for the remainder of the weekend. I was surrounded by death, like it was an old friend: a sad friend, but at least a loyal one.

That weekend was the nudge I needed – the push to turn the page and finally move on.

The notice period was 12 weeks, but I had enough leave and days in lieu to take the last 4 weeks off. Those 8 weeks were strange. Some colleagues were sad to see me go, and I was sorry to leave them. Some didn't mention it at all, maybe a defence mechanism?

And some were angry, though I never truly understood why. Perhaps, chasing my dream reminded some of my workmates of the ones they had abandoned. At the time, it hurt. Now, I pray for them. Everyone is on their own journey, doing the best they can at any given moment, me included.

I've never been good at goodbyes. My last few shifts were nights, and when the final one ended, I simply walked into a new day – a new chapter.

I disappeared overnight to start a new life.

By January 2023, I had become a different person. I had shed the weight of who I was and emerged as something new – an entrepreneur. Like a butterfly finally breaking free from its cocoon.

Do I regret leaving? No.

Do I miss medicine? No.

Would I have done it sooner? Yes.

Why I Chose the Bold Leap

Looking back, I see now that my choice was what Dr Onu describes in Chapter 4 as the Bold Leap. I didn't ease my way out slowly or hold onto a safety net – I let go entirely and built something new from the ground up. And while a Quiet Pivot might have preserved more stability, for me, it was the Bold Leap that gave me the freedom to embrace the life I was being called into fully.

Life Now

Today, my life is entirely different. I still carry the discipline, skills, and perspective medicine gave me, but now I have the freedom and creativity I craved for so long.

I've built multiple streams of income, a global community, and a lifestyle that allows me to work on my own terms.

Most importantly, I've found alignment again. A way of living and working that makes my soul sing.

I've built my rich life.

Lessons for Others

Here's what I've learned along the way:

1. Listen to the whispers. Your soul will always nudge you when something is off. Don't ignore it.

2. Support matters. Even a small circle of people who believe in you can change everything.

3. Fear is part of the process. Doubt doesn't mean you're on the wrong path; it means you're growing.

4. Small wins build considerable momentum. Don't wait for the perfect plan; start where you are, start small, and build up your big dream one brick at a time.

5. Your past doesn't define your future. What you've done until now doesn't limit what you can create next.

I want you to remember this: "Reinvention isn't about throwing away who you were. It's about expanding into who you're meant to become."

Short Biography

Dr Ola van Steen is a physician-turned-travel entrepreneur who transitioned from the high-pressure world of Intensive Care and acute medicine to building a thriving global travel enterprise. She now inspires others to design lives of freedom and alignment.

Connect with her at: https://linkedin.com/in/drolaabbas.

Summary

Dr Ola's story is a reminder we all need sometimes – you don't have to burn yourself out to be "successful." You don't have to keep running just because that's what everyone expects.

She chose courage over comfort, and in doing that, she built the life of her dreams.

That's the real heart of reinvention. It's not about throwing everything away and starting from scratch. It's about leaning into who you were always meant to be.

And as we move on, you're about to dive into another story in the next chapter. A whole new journey. Different struggles. Fresh lessons. But the same unstoppable power that shows up when you decide it's time for something new.

Trust me, you don't want to miss this one, so keep reading, it's going to hit home!

CHAPTER 9: FROM A HOUSEBOY TO A GLOBAL INFLUENCER – DR IFEANYI AKALEME'S BECOMING

Trigger Warning

This chapter contains descriptions of poverty, adversity, loss, and emotional challenges. If you feel distressed, please pause and seek support from a trusted health professional or helpline.

> *"Kings are still made from the trenches, so it doesn't matter your background or what you have been through"*
>
> – Ifeanyi Akaleme

Some stories remind us that no matter how far back life seems to push you, there's always a way forward. Dr Ifeanyi Akaleme's journey is one such story. It's a story of pain, rejection, resilience, and eventually – **Reinvention**.

From starting life in poverty and servitude to building a global brand that impacts nations, his story proves that your past doesn't define your future. As you read, notice how each stage of his story connects back to the **7 Steps of Reinvention**. This isn't just a story;

it's proof that reinvention is possible, regardless of your background.

The Call That Changed Everything

It was a Thursday morning in August 2021. I was on my way to work when my phone rang. On the other end was my Human Resources officer.

"Ifeanyi, you have been sacked," she said abruptly. "Please come and pick up your letter from my office."

I froze. For a few seconds, I couldn't breathe. I had read about people losing their jobs in books. I had seen it happen in movies. But me? Fired? That was never something I thought would happen.

Just a week earlier, I had been rushed from one meeting to another. It felt like I was on trial for crimes I didn't even understand – accused of things I would never have done.

Without knowing it, I had been sucked into the dark, toxic underbelly of workplace politics. And at the centre of it all was my manager, who seemed determined to erase me from our organisation at all costs.

I was being manipulated, set up for a downfall. A slow execution, corporate style. Some might call it the ugly side of the workplace, but for me, it was a nightmare I never saw coming.

Quitting never crossed my mind. I was tender, inexperienced, and maybe a little too naïve. Yet, in the middle of all that chaos, something unexpected was being birthed. This very pain, this very betrayal, became the vehicle for my rediscovery.

Back to the Beginning: a Childhood in Lack

I didn't just stumble into hardship at work; I was raised in it.

My earliest memories as a child, aged five or six, were filled with hunger, sickness, and poverty. I often wondered if life was supposed to be so cruel. Sometimes I asked myself: Was everyone born just to suffer?

We didn't just live in poverty; we lived in abject, pit-bottom poverty: No food, no clothes, no roof we could call ours. Many times, I watched as my family was thrown out of mud houses in the village because we couldn't pay rent.

My mother was always gone, trading endlessly just to ensure we had something – anything – to eat. My father, an uneducated pastor, worked tirelessly on the farm because the church could not pay him enough to support us. As the last child, all I wanted was my mother's presence. But by the time I was four, I already knew she would never be around in the way I longed for.

The Escape: Choosing Hardship Over Comfort

By age seven, something inside me erupted. It was my first "if I perish, I perish" moment. I packed my few clothes into a sack bag and walked to a church member's house in the city, not as a guest, but as a houseboy.

I spent seventeen years of my life in servitude. Years of shame, abuse, rejection, and isolation. But also, years where I built resilience without even knowing it.

Yet, nothing prepared me for the day I lost my job as an adult.

This time, resilience wasn't enough. The pain of losing my job cut deeper than I imagined. The shame of facing my peers, of standing before colleagues who once saw me as capable. It broke me in ways I didn't expect. And in the middle of it all was one haunting question: "How do I feed my aged mother?"

Yet, in that valley of sorrow and silence, something new was born. Out of the ashes of rejection, in 2022 I founded my first company, **Project Nations** – a seed planted after surviving a whole year without structured employment.

A Calling Forged in Poverty

Did I have a career before the detour? Absolutely.

From an early age, I carried a mandate: a vision to liberate my family and my entire lineage from poverty.

It was sometime in 1997 when I made that decision. That year became the turning point, where I vowed to eradicate poverty from my family forever. My story felt much like that of biblical Joseph – called to something bigger, but only after enduring hardship.

I began to notice something unique about myself – that I possessed a high adversity quotient – a stubborn will to win that my siblings didn't seem to carry. Once I stepped out of my mother's house, I felt a strange resonance, as if I was being pulled by something greater.

I was young. I was inexperienced. But I was determined. That decision marked my first moment of stepping out of my comfort zone and into the unknown. It was like being called into dark oceans, like walking on deep waters without knowing if I would sink.

And so, I went.

What followed was a childhood and adolescence marked by abuse, depression, deprivation, rejection, isolation, and loneliness. Words can only scratch the surface; some of those emotions are now buried too deep even to describe.

I moved in with a church member's family in Umuahia, Nigeria – the very church where my father pastored. But instead of being welcomed, I was rejected.

The wife of that church member never wanted me around; she made it clear with words that cut deeply. Her rejection starved me of love, made me feel unwanted; yet I endured, and I stayed. I had made myself a promise: I wasn't going back to my mother's house, no matter what.

So, I stayed.

Resilience was forged in those years. I found strength in rejection and isolation.

The Turning Point

Fast forward to 30 July 2025.

The eruption came. Not the kind that destroys, but the kind that forges, moulds, and amplifies. A volcanic eruption that birthed a new me – a global leader in the making, destined to stand before nations.

Just a day before, a beautiful Tuesday morning, I was the star boy: Group Head of the healthcare sector at a multinational commercial bank in Nigeria. I had the salary, the car, the apartment – everything that looked glamorous from the outside.

But inside? I was empty.

That wasn't the future I had endured hardship for. Every morning, I woke with a void, a darkness I couldn't shake. On that Wednesday morning, the fire inside me reached boiling point. My line manager unknowingly triggered the eruption that had been building for years.

The Leap

All through my career, one thing remained constant: I carried a passion for excellence.

A spirit that refused to tolerate mediocrity, no matter who brought it.

At every stage in the corporate world, I found myself fighting mediocrity, ambiguity, and obscurity. I challenged broken systems. I confronted processes that rewarded lip service instead of creativity, systems that applauded vain loyalty while stifling innovation and productivity.

Sometimes, that drive for excellence made people admire me. At other times, it made them dislike me. Some bosses perceived my openness and courage in calling out flawed leadership as a threat to them.

But all along, it was a clue – a whisper of what I was truly called to do: to raise leaders, leaders who would transform Africa and their communities across the world. Leaders who would live differently, lead differently, and build legacies.

On 30 July 2025, I pressed "send" and submitted my resignation letter.

And immediately, the weight lifted, and I felt a sense of freedom. That day, I said no to suppression. I said no to mediocrity.

But more importantly, I said "yes".

- Yes to building the life of my dreams.
- Yes to creating something meaningful.
- Yes to soaring like an eagle to the nations.
- Yes to freedom.
- Yes to raising unstoppable leaders.
- Yes to impacting nations across the globe.

That was the day I realised I had been preparing for it all along, from the hungry boy carrying a sack bag to serve as a houseboy, to the man who dared to walk away from comfort in pursuit of purpose.

Early Challenges and Wins

When I stepped out, I didn't step out empty. I stepped out as a global leader, a two-time founder, an entrepreneur, a sales expert, a business manager, a lifestyle strategist, a lover, and a dreamer.

I didn't begin at level zero. I started at level one.

Of course, building a global organization from almost nothing would not be easy. But I carried with me fifteen years of experience across multiple sectors. Every lesson, every scar, every win – all of it was fuel for this new chapter.

The very next morning, 31 July 2025, I woke up to a new reality. I had just assumed full leadership of a team of twenty remote staff whom I'd hired to work in my second startup, The Hunt, only two months before leaving my paid employment. No-one handed me a manual. No boss was standing over me. It was just me: my vision, and the people who believed enough to come on board.

Suddenly, I wasn't just managing my employer's brand: I was managing mine. I wasn't selling someone else's products: I was selling mine. And that ocean of freedom? It was exhilarating.

Yet the detours still existed; the people's problems remained. However, I have developed the skills to manage people throughout my years of employment.

Thanks to my global influence and network, a community that has now become my support system, I was able to onboard investors and clients early. We signed global contracts when most people thought we were still "just starting".

Reading back over my story, I now see how much of it reflects what Dr Onu explains in Chapter 6: cultural and family expectations. My early battles weren't just about poverty or pain – they were about voices telling me who I could or couldn't become. Learning to sift through those voices and choosing my own path was the fundamental reinvention.

Life Now

For me, the son of Akaleme, a poor man who passed on but planted a seed of greatness in me, this is the life I always dreamed of.

A life filled with vision.

A life of freedom and creativity.

A life of giving back to nations and to my community every single day.

Years ago, I dreamed of being able to vacation anywhere, at any time. Today, that's a reality. I have my first trip lined up to Kigali,

Rwanda, for a tech convention, followed by another to Doha, Qatar, to meet with business associates.

As I write this, I've signed a lifetime research project with a Nigerian celebrity, proof that even my passion for academia still has room to shine.

I've founded not one, but two startups:

- **Project Nations**: leading a revolution in strategic business management and consulting across Africa.

- **The Hunt Nigeria**: the first-of-its-kind singles marketplace designed specifically for Africans.

And beyond that, I've stepped into my calling as a lifestyle marketer and branding expert, closing seven-figure deals that remind me daily that freedom pays.

Indeed, this is just the beginning.

The village boy who once carried a sack bag to serve as a houseboy has now become a man serving nations. And if there's one truth my journey has taught me, it's this: You don't wait for the right time to step into your future. You create the right time, and the future unfolds.

Lessons for Others

Before you pivot:

1. Have a five-year plan: It might sound demanding but stretch yourself. Map out a solid yet flexible plan in five key areas: Relationships, Education, Career Growth, Investment, and Social Impact or Spirituality.

2. Do a self-audit: Twice a year, assess your progress against your five-year plan. This simple ritual gives you clarity on where you are and where you're headed.

3. Find a mentor who embodies your goals: Nothing is new under the sun. Seek out someone who resonates with your vision. Even if you can't connect with them directly, study their journey – read their profiles, note the courses they took, the programs they attended, and replicate wisely.

4. Build or join a community: No one succeeds in isolation. Either create your own circle of growth or join one that aligns with your goals.

5. Take your personal branding seriously: If you don't tell your story, others will – but not the way you'd want it said. This is your time to show the world who you're becoming. You don't need to be perfect, just intentional. Choose a platform, use a picture that reflects your story, and start sharing your presence.

In summary: Don't wait for perfect timing or conditions; they don't exist. Step out with faith and determination. Tell the universe, "I can do this. I have the capacity, even when I don't feel ready."

> *"Fear is not the absence of faith; unbelief is. You can do it afraid."*
>
> *– Ifeanyi Akaleme*

> *"You were crushed for a purpose, because you have content. You could not fit in because you have a calling. It is because you're a raw material and the universe is moulding you into that purpose and shape that will transform lives."*
>
> *– Ifeanyi Akaleme*

Move, but only forward.

Short Biography

Dr Ifeanyi Akaleme is a houseboy turned banker who transitioned from the corporate banking industry to founding and building two startups in lifestyle management and business consulting. Ifeanyi inspires thousands of young people worldwide through his transformational stories.

Connect with him here: https://www.linkedin.com/in/ifeanyi-akaleme.

Summary

Dr Akaleme's journey reminds us that where you start doesn't have to be where you end. From being a houseboy to becoming a global influencer, his story is living proof that even the darkest beginnings can give birth to the brightest futures.

He chose to rise when life tried to bury him. He chose purpose over comfort, faith over fear, and that choice created the freedom and impact he walks in today. That's the true power of reinvention: not erasing your past but transforming it into the fuel for your future.

And just when you think you've seen it all, the following story comes in with a whole new twist. Different struggles. Different lessons. But the same undeniable truth: **you can become more**.

Keep reading. The next chapter is about to shake something inside you.

CHAPTER 10: FROM STAY-AT-HOME MUM TO GLOBAL INFLUENCE – EMILY WALE-KOYA'S JOURNEY

Trigger Warning

This chapter contains descriptions of poverty, adversity, loss, and emotional challenges. If you feel distressed, please pause and seek support from a trusted health professional or helpline.

> *"Reinvention doesn't wait for you to be ready. It demands you start before you feel qualified."*
>
> – Emily Wale-Koya

Some stories don't just inspire you; they wake you up. Emily Wale-Koya's story is one of those.

It's the story of a young mum who found herself drowning in bills, debt, and self-doubt, yet somehow turned her dining table into a launchpad for global influence. She could have surrendered. Instead, she chose to rewrite her story.

From a broke, timid, stay-at-home mum in Nigeria to becoming one of Africa's most sought-after personal branding coaches with a global footprint, her journey is proof that sometimes, your lowest point is actually your launchpad.

She wasn't "prepared." She didn't even have a roadmap. But she had the **hunger**, **grit**, and the **courage** to say: "Enough. Something has to change."

And that decision? It didn't just shift her life. It reinvented her completely.

The Awakening

I can still picture it as if it were yesterday.

I was at my dining table with my newborn on one arm, breastfeeding, while my other hand tapped away on my laptop. Bills were scattered everywhere. Rent was due. School fees were unpaid. For the first time, we were in debt.

At that moment, it hit me hard: this cannot be my life.

Up until then, my income had always been tied to my husband's contracts. When his business dried up, mine followed suit. Suddenly, everything shifted. I felt like I was standing at a crossroads, with nothing but my children's future staring me in the face. Something had to move quickly. I had to wake the hell up.

Backstory

Unlike most people, I never had the typical 9-to-5 path and never really had a "career ladder" to climb. After university, I held only one job, working as the owner's personal assistant at a restaurant. After that? I became a full-time stay-at-home mum.

Not because it was my dream. But because life just unfolded that way.

I did what was expected. I took what came.

However, after having three children, the cracks began to show. I loved my family deeply, but I couldn't shake the restlessness inside me. I wanted more. I wanted to matter outside of diapers, school runs, and unpaid bills.

The truth? I was broke, unfulfilled, and questioning who I was becoming.

The Turning Point

One day, in the middle of breastfeeding sessions and mounting bills, I made a decision.

I was no longer going to let life just happen to me.

I may not have had money. I may not have had a blueprint. But I had something more powerful – my story, my voice, and a burning desire to help women like me.

That decision led to the creation of my first online course, **Passion to Profit Mastery**, in 2016.

It was rough. Messy. Unpolished. But it was mine.

And the wild part? I launched it, sold it, and made it profitable before I even finished creating the course.

That was all I needed. The proof that I could rewrite my story.

The Leap

Now, let me be honest with you: I was once the most timid girl in any room.

I feared being seen. I doubted myself constantly.

But reinvention doesn't wait for you to be ready. It demands you start right where you are, with what you have.

So, I showed up online anyway.

I recorded shaky videos.

I posted imperfect content.

I continued to learn, fail, and try again.

And every time I pressed "publish," I wasn't just sharing content – I was rebuilding myself – piece by piece.

Early Challenges and Small Wins

Was it easy? Absolutely not.

Many people didn't believe that someone from Nigeria could build a legitimate online business. I had no investors, no connections, and no roadmap.

But I kept showing up anyway.

And slowly, the wins started to roll in.

- ➢ My first paying client.
- ➢ My first small online community.

> The messages from women saying, "Emily, your story inspired me."

The day someone paid me for what I already knew was the day I realised – my experience was valuable, and it could pay the bills.

My Support

Behind every reinvention story, there's usually someone who believed in you before you believed in yourself. For me, that person was, without a doubt, my pastor.

For over 20 years, he poured personal development and leadership training into me. His teachings opened my eyes to fight for my life and to design the future I wanted. He inspired me to go after what was possible for me when everything around me said it wasn't.

My pastor became like the father I didn't have. He even showed up where my biological father couldn't. He trained me spiritually, raised me with discipline and hope, and reminded me that my voice mattered long before I ever found the courage to use it.

That support gave me the strength to face my fears, to keep showing up online. It turned my shaky beginnings into solid ground. Without my pastor's support, I wouldn't have had the resilience to press "publish" on those early videos or the faith to keep going when the road felt impossibly hard.

I'm eternally grateful to my pastor.

Looking back, I now see what Dr Onu describes in Chapter 5: the power of a Support Circle. My pastor was my Guide – offering wisdom, training, and belief in me when I couldn't yet believe in myself. And that made all the difference.

Life Now

Fast forward to today, and that timid, broke stay-at-home mum has become a global voice.

- I've coached over 25,000 people worldwide.
- I've spoken at more than 100 events, including TEDx.
- I've built a social media community of more than 350,000 followers.
- I've founded the **School of Personal Branding**, helping CEOs, founders, and professionals build powerful brands.
- I've worked with clients in the US, UK, Ireland, Canada, Dubai, France, and across Africa – all from my home in Port Harcourt, Nigeria.

And I'm just getting started.

Soon, I'll be launching a world-class learning platform and community for Africans at home and abroad. A place where they can take control of their lives, build powerhouse brands, charge their worth, and future-proof their careers.

For 9 years now, I've built my business from the same place it started: my dining table. While raising four children, I've also raised a brand that touches lives across the globe.

That's what reinvention looks like.

Lessons for Others

If you're standing at a crossroads, here's what my journey has taught me and what I want you to learn from:

- ➤ Reinvention doesn't wait for perfect timing. It starts the moment you decide.

- ➤ You don't need an office. You don't even need permission. You can start from your dining table.

- ➤ Your story is your power. Package it. Share it. Let it open doors for you.

- ➤ Reinvention isn't just about changing careers. It's about changing who you believe you are.

- ➤ Consistency makes you undeniable. Keep showing up, even when you're scared.

If a broke, timid, stay-at-home mum from Nigeria could reinvent herself into a global influence, then so can you.

Because the blueprint for reinvention isn't only hidden in a book, a job, or a title. It's already inside **you.** Waiting for you to choose it.

Short Biography

Emily Wale-Koya is a stay-at-home mum turned global personal branding strategist. From her dining table in Port Harcourt, while raising her newborn baby, she built a business that has coached over 25,000 people worldwide. Today, she runs the **School of Personal Branding** and continues to inspire thousands with her reinvention story.

Connect with her here: https://www.linkedin.com/in/emily-wale-koya.

Summary

Emily Wale-Koya's story is proof that reinvention isn't reserved for the privileged. It's available to anyone willing to say, "I'm not staying here. I'm becoming more."

From a broke, timid stay-at-home mum to a global influence, Emily shows us that the comfort of your home can be your launchpad. Your voice can be your vehicle, and your story can be your power.

The question is, will you **choose** to use it?

Because like Emily, reinvention isn't just about your career, it's about transforming yourself.

And yet, as powerful as career reinvention is, there's a bigger question waiting just beyond the horizon: what happens when the career chapter closes?

We've now walked through the seven steps of reinvention and explored real-life stories from leaders across the globe. But before this journey ends, there's one more conversation we must have – one that shifts the focus from **success today** to **impact tomorrow**.

That's what Chapter 11 is about: **Legacy Beyond Retirement**.

Because reinvention isn't only about what you do next, it's about what you leave behind.

PART 3

THE FUTURE – LIVING AND LEAVING A LEGACY

Reinvention isn't just about changing your life –
it's about shaping the lives that follow.

CHAPTER 11: LEGACY BEYOND RETIREMENT – REINVENTING FOR PURPOSE AND IMPACT

"Retirement isn't the end of impact – it's the beginning of reinvention, on your terms."

– Dr David Onu

We've spent this book walking through 7 steps of reinvention. You've seen how real people – from surgeons to entrepreneurs, from leaders to stay-at-home mums – found the courage to pivot and create work that fits their evolving selves.

But reinvention doesn't end when your career does. In fact, for many, it's only the beginning of a new kind of impact.

This is the chapter about **Legacy**.

Reinvention isn't only about climbing to the next level, getting the next role, or launching the next venture. It's about asking:

- ➢ What will remain after I'm gone?

- ➢ How will my wisdom, my values, and my story ripple into the lives of others?

- ➢ What kind of footprints am I leaving behind?

For some, retirement feels like a closing door. But for those who embrace legacy, it becomes a wide-open highway – a season where contribution is no longer limited by job titles, Key Performance Indicators, or even age.

Here, we'll explore how to reinvent with legacy in mind. You'll see how purpose can outlive pay-checks, how meaning can stretch beyond milestones, and how the impact of a life well-lived continues long after the work is done.

A Colleague's Honest Words

> *"Retirement was not going well for me."*

That was the candid message I received from a respected colleague not long ago. After decades as a health leader, he had stepped into retirement, only to find it unfulfilling.

So, when the chance came to return to an academic teaching role, he jumped at it.

Not for the money. Not for the prestige.

But because doing nothing was draining him more than doing something.

His honesty made me pause and wonder:

- ➢ What truly makes retirement fulfilling for some, yet frustrating for others?
- ➢ Is it the sudden quiet after a lifetime of activity?
- ➢ Is it the struggle to find identity beyond job titles?
- ➢ Or is it perhaps the absence of a clear sense of purpose?

Here's what I believe:

> *"Retirement is not the end of the road; it is the beginning of the open highway."*

Why This Chapter Matters

This chapter is not another step in the reinvention process. It's a reminder that reinvention doesn't expire. Whether you're thirty or seventy, the need to live with purpose never stops.

Retirement doesn't end your story; instead, it opens a new one, one where impact outweighs titles and freedom meets contribution.

It's about asking yourself:

- What legacy do I want to leave behind?
- How can I use my skills and experience to make a difference?
- How do I want to be remembered, not for what I had, but for what I gave?

Your answers shape the quality of your reinvention in later life.

And here's the beauty of it – legacy isn't only about what you leave behind when you're gone. It's shaped by how you live now. Every choice, every conversation, every seed you plant in others becomes part of the story you'll be remembered for.

Which brings us to the heart of it all: how do you actually build a legacy that outlives you?

How to Build a Legacy That Outlives You

The ultimate reward of reinvention isn't just financial stability or a fresh career path. It's bigger than that. It's the chance to create something that echoes long after you're gone. That's what true legacy is about.

One of the most profound illustrations of this truth is found in Will Allen Dromgoole's timeless poem "The Bridge Builder".

In the poem, an older man crosses a dangerous chasm safely, but instead of walking away, he stops to build a bridge. A fellow traveller questions him, pointing out that he will never need the bridge again. The older man responds that he is not building it for himself but for the young travellers who will come after him, for whom the chasm may be a stumbling block.

This imagery is powerful. Legacy is not about the bridges you crossed for yourself; it's about the ones you build for others.

Just like the older man, future generations may not measure your most significant impact in what you gained for yourself, but in the paths, you cleared and the bridges you built for others. That is legacy in action.

It's less about what you hand over, and more about the seeds you plant in people. Seeds that keep growing even when you're no longer here.

So, how do you shape a legacy like that?

1. Pass down your wisdom

Don't only share your victories, share the challenges too. Tell the stories of the times you failed, the lessons that shaped you, and the truths that anchored you. Write them down, record them, or sit with someone younger to talk. Because when you open up about the road you've walked, you make it easier for those coming after you to walk theirs without stumbling in the same places.

2. Mentor someone

There's always someone a step or two behind you. Someone who hasn't faced the challenges you've faced but may. That may be your colleague, a younger sibling, or even a stranger who looks up to you quietly. Your scars, your lessons, your comebacks, they're not just for you. They're a map someone else desperately needs. Be generous with it. Sometimes your story is the very thing that lights another person's path.

3. Strengthen family traditions

Legacy isn't always built in the big, flashy moments; it often lives in the quiet, ordinary moments we share. The Sunday meals where laughter fills the room. The prayer that brings everyone's hearts together before the day begins or ends. That one tradition you repeat every year that makes everyone feel like they belong.

These little things might seem small, but over time, they become the glue that holds the family together. They remind us of where we come from and give those after us something steady to lean on.

Here's a gentle question for you: What traditions are you nurturing today that could become tomorrow's anchor for your family?

4. Extend your impact to the community

Your reinvention isn't just for you. It's for others, too. The moment you start pouring into your community, whether by serving, volunteering, or creating opportunities, you multiply your impact.

That's when your story stops being just about you and starts becoming a gift to others.

5. Document your journey

Every life holds a story worth telling, **yours included**. The battles you've fought, the lessons you've carved out of pain, the victories you've celebrated – those aren't random experiences. They are chapters of wisdom that can light the path for someone else.

According to Benjamin Franklin,

"If you would not be forgotten, as soon as you are dead and rotten, either write things worth reading, or do things worth writing."

Don't let your life experiences and wisdom fade away. Put them into words. It might be in the form of a book that carries your story, a journal that becomes a treasure, or a podcast that reaches strangers across the world. Whatever the form, your story deserves a voice.

One day, someone might stumble across your words and feel the exact hope they've been searching for. That's the beauty of documenting your journey – your voice keeps speaking, even when you're not in the room.

It's one of the reasons I chose to write this book. Not just for me, but for the people I may never meet, the ones who might need the very lessons my journey has taught me. And I believe the same for you. Your story could be the one that shifts someone's perspective, lifts their spirit, or even changes the course of their life.

Pause and Reflect

- What does retirement mean to you? Simply relaxing on the beach and stepping away from all "meaningful" work, or an opportunity to continue contributing in ways that matter in your free time?

- Do you genuinely need to retire? Although a retirement age exists, some professions, such as the medical field, permit individuals to continue working well beyond that milestone.

- Are you genuinely prepared for retirement – financially, emotionally, and in terms of purpose?

The Benefits and Risks of Retirement

Retirement can be a season of freedom and rediscovery. It offers time to pursue passions you may have put on hold – activities such as deepening relationships, travelling, or engaging in meaningful projects that align with your values. It can also provide a welcome break from work-related stress and an opportunity to focus on your health, wellbeing, and personal growth.

At the same time, retirement carries potential risks. Some individuals may struggle with a loss of career identity or purpose, feeling restless or disconnected when they are no longer part of the work structure. Social isolation can creep in if daily interactions diminish, and financial pressures may emerge if planning hasn't been adequate.

Being aware of both the benefits and risks of retirement allows you to plan intentionally. It ensures that the retirement phase becomes one of fulfillment, impact, and meaningful contribution.

Summary

Retirement is not an ending, but a reinvention —a season where freedom and purpose align to create lasting influence. True legacy is not postponed until you're gone; it is shaped in the present through the choices you make and the lives you touch.

This chapter outlines five ways to build a lasting legacy: share your wisdom, mentor others, strengthen family traditions, invest in your community, and document your journey. Each step transforms experience into impact, ensuring your life continues to inspire and guide others long after you have passed on.

Retirement, then, is more than stepping away from work. It is an opportunity to redefine significance, expand influence, and write the next chapter with meaning.

FINAL THOUGHT: YOU ARE RIGHT ON TIME – EMBRACING YOUR NEXT CHAPTER FULLY

"It's never too late to be what you might have been."

– George Eliot

Society has a way of pressuring us with invisible timelines: graduate by a certain age, build a career by another age, have it all figured out before a specific number on the calendar. And when we don't "measure up," we start believing we're behind. However, reinvention doesn't adhere to those rules. It follows your pace, your journey, and your truth.

It is not about erasing your past, but about transforming it into the very foundation of what comes next. Reinvention is the decision to honour your becoming – to expand into your highest purpose, and to allow your talents and experiences to unfold in newer and fuller ways.

I once worked with a woman in her early fifties who felt it was "too late" to reinvent her career. She carried the weight of believing that starting over meant she had failed. But when she began to let go of those limiting beliefs, everything shifted. She discovered her age wasn't a barrier at all – it was her most significant advantage. Her wisdom, resilience, and hard-earned life experience became the very traits that set her apart.

That shift opened the door to a new career in counselling, where her depth of experience became her superpower and the reason she could help others so powerfully.

Her story is a reminder: you are not behind. You are not late. You are not early. You are right on time. This moment – right here, right now – is the perfect time to begin again, to align with your purpose, and to step boldly into the next chapter of your life.

George Washington Carver admonishes us to:

> *"Start where you are, with what you have. Make something of it and never be satisfied."*

Reflection

- ➤ What beliefs about timing have been holding you back?

- ➤ How would your story change if you began to see this very moment as the right time to start?

CAREER REINVENTION TOOLKIT – PRACTICAL STEPS TO ALIGN YOUR LIFE AND CAREER

"Vision without action is a daydream. Action without vision is a nightmare."

– Japanese proverb

Before we part ways, I don't just want to leave you with ideas; I want to leave you with tools.

Think of this toolkit as a compass and a map for your journey of reinvention.

Use it to gain clarity, challenge old beliefs, and take practical steps toward the life you've been imagining. These exercises aren't homework, they're steppingstones.

Clarity Prompts

Sometimes the answers you're searching for are already inside; you just need the right questions to draw them out.

Reflect deeply and honestly:

- What parts of your current career energise you?

- Which parts drain you or feel misaligned with your purpose?

- If there were no limitations, what would you pursue?

- Describe your ideal workday. How closely does your current routine match it?

- What strengths do you carry that aren't being used to their full potential?

Values Alignment Worksheets

When your work doesn't match your values, it always feels heavier than it should. This 4-step exercise helps you lighten that load.

Step 1: Identify Core Values

Write down your top five personal core values:

1. _____

2. _____

3. _____

4. _____

5. _____

Not sure where to start? Here are a few values people often prioritise:

- Service to others

- Adventure and lifestyle (travel, new experiences)
- Family and close relationships
- Career growth and impact
- Financial security and stability

Yours may look different, and that's perfectly okay. Write down what feels most important to you right now, in this season of life.

Remember, values can shift as you grow. Early-career professionals may focus on career growth, while later in their careers, they may prioritise family, service, or lifestyle. Whatever they are, your top five values aren't just words on a page – they're your compass. The more precise you are here, the easier it becomes to recognise the paths that fit you and to say "no" to the ones that don't.

Step 2: Evaluate Career Alignment

For each value above, rate how well your current career aligns (1 = Not at all, 5 = Completely).

Value 1: _____

Value 2: _____

Value 3: _____

Value 4: _____

Value 5: _____

Step 3: Spot the Gaps

- ➤ Where do you see misalignment?
- ➤ How might this explain your restlessness?

Step 4: Realignment Plan

Write down specific actions you can take to bring your career closer to your values.

Action 1: _____

Action 2: _____

Action 3: _____

Mindset Audit Exercises

Most of the limits we face aren't external; they live in our own heads. Let's rewrite those stories, using a 2-step exercise.

Step 1: Identify Your Limiting Beliefs

Write down three beliefs that have been holding you back from your career decisions.

1. _____

2. _____

3. _____

Step 2: Challenge and Reframe

For each belief above, challenge its validity and reframe it positively:

- Original belief: _____

- Evidence against this belief:
  _____

- New empowering belief:
  _____

Example:

Original belief: "I'm too old to start over."

Evidence against it: "Many people start new careers at 50, 60, even 70."

New empowering belief: "My age is my advantage – it gives me wisdom and resilience."

Repeat this often. The more you challenge the old story, the weaker it becomes.

Planning Templates

Dreams don't become reality by accident. That is where clarity meets action. Use the 4-step template below.

Step 1: Define Your Goal (the SMART Way)

➤ *Write your reinvention goal clearly.*

_____

Clarity is everything. A vague goal like "I want a better career" won't get you far.

Instead, use the **SMART** framework to make your goal Specific, Measurable, Achievable, Relevant, and Time-bound.

The SMART framework:

- ➤ **Specific**: What exactly do you want to achieve? Avoid vague terms like "better" or "more."

- ➤ **Measurable**: How will you know when you've achieved it? Define success in clear terms.

- ➤ **Achievable**: Is it realistic, given your resources, skills, and circumstances?

- ➤ **Relevant**: Does it align with your deeper values, priorities, and season of life?

- ➤ **Time-bound**: What's your timeframe? Give yourself a deadline to create focus and urgency.

Example:

Vague Goal: "I want to start my own business someday."

SMART Goal: "Within the next 9 months, I will launch an online graphic design consultancy that serves at least three paying clients, generates a minimum monthly income of $2,000, and allows me to work remotely so I can spend more time with my family."

Step 2: Milestones and Timelines

Break your goal into manageable milestones and assign realistic deadlines:

Milestone 1: _____

Deadline: _____

Milestone 2: _____

Deadline: _____

Milestone 3: _____

Deadline: _____

Step 3: Resources and Support

List the resources and people you'll need around you to succeed.

Resource 1: _____

Resource 2: _____

Support network: _____

Step 4: Track Your Progress

Schedule regular weekly reviews and monthly reflections to ensure ongoing progress. Adjust your plan as needed.

Weekly review date/time:
_____

Monthly reflection date/time: _____

ACKNOWLEDGEMENTS

This book is the fruit of many seeds sown into my life, and I honour those who watered them.

To God

I give thanks to Almighty God for the gift of life and a sound mind, which enabled me to complete this project.

To My Family

Your unwavering belief in me turned long nights into meaningful mornings. Chinyere – your unwavering support and understanding made space for this dream to take form. Zoronachi, Chidiamara, Olaedo, and Nneoma – thank you for reminding me that true success begins and ends with love.

To My Parents

To my late father, HRH Eze David Aba Onu, whose integrity, resilience, and service continue to guide my path, and to my late mother, Enyidiya Uzo Onu, whose faith and generosity profoundly shaped me – thank you for the foundation you laid. I am because you were.

To My Collaborators and Contributors

Special thanks to Dr Ikechukwu Okoh for writing the inspiring foreword of this book, and to Dr Ola van Steen, Dr Ifeanyi Akaleme PhD, and Emily Wale-Koya for generously sharing their stories of reinvention. Your honesty and lived experiences have brought depth and authenticity to this blueprint. I'm also grateful to the early readers who offered helpful feedback and reviews.

To My Mentors and Friends

I also acknowledge my mentors, friends, and coaches who sharpened my vision and refined my calling. Special thanks to my branding coach, whose clarity session sparked the framework that became this book, and to every voice that challenged me to align work with purpose.

To My Readers and Community

Finally, to you – my readers, newsletter subscribers, and online community – thank you for walking this journey with me. Your questions, reflections, and feedback have made this work richer, deeper, and more relevant.

A note to the reader. This is a shared journey: from restless to realigned, from success to significance. If this book has helped you pause, reflect, or take one courageous step, you're already walking the path of reinvention.

REFERENCES FOR FURTHER READING

Herzberg's Two-Factor Theory

Herzberg, F. (1959). *The Motivation to Work*. New York: John Wiley.

For an accessible overview: Nickerson, C. (2025). "Herzberg's Two-Factor Theory of Motivation." *Simply Psychology*. https://www.simplypsychology.org/herzbergs-two-factor-theory.html

Growth vs Fixed Mindset

Dweck, C. S. (2006). *Mindset: The New Psychology of Success*. Random House.

See also: "Implicit theories of intelligence." In *Wikipedia*. https://en.m.wikipedia.org/wiki/Implicit_theories_of_intelligence

Harvard Study of Adult Development

Mineo, Liz (2023). "Work out daily? OK, but how socially fit are you?" *Harvard Gazette*. https://news.harvard.edu/gazette/story/2023/02/work-out-daily-ok-but-how-socially-fit-are-you/

Ten Areas of Life

Onu, D. (2022). "Ten areas of life you require for successful living." https://davidonu.com/areas-of-life/

INVITE ME TO SPEAK AT YOUR NEXT EVENT

If this book resonated with you, imagine sharing its message with your team or audience.

I am available to speak with leaders to grow deeper, lead with heart, and reinvent their lives with clarity and confidence.

I inspire audiences to pause, realign, and pursue the life and work they were truly meant for-- with courage, purpose, and renewed direction.

Scan the QR code below, visit www.DavidOnu.com/speaking to connect.

SIGNATURE TOPICS

- ✓ Career Reinvention
- ✓ Personal & Career Growth
- ✓ Nurturing Relationships
- ✓ Self-Care & Work-Life Balance
- ✓ Keynotes & Panels
- ✓ Guest Appearances

"You were absolutely brilliant. Thank you for tying the whole day together so beautifully!"
- Angela Driver CEO TLP.

ABOUT THE AUTHOR

Dr David Onu (MBBS, MForensMed, FACLM, FRACGP, GTLP), is a medical specialist and internationally certified Results, Relationship, Life, and Career Reinvention Coach. Over a 26-year career spanning Nigeria, the Caribbean, and Australia, he has guided countless professionals and leaders to rediscover clarity, balance, and purpose.

After stepping away from a demanding surgical path to realign his life with his core values, David's journey of reinvention became both his message and mission. Today, he serves as a Clinical Associate Professor at the University of Tasmania Medical School and leads statewide health transformation within the Tasmanian Health Service.

Through his *Grow and Lead* newsletter, coaching, and speaking engagements, David combines medical insight with emotional intelligence to help value-driven professionals reinvent their careers and lives with courage and compassion.

He lives in Tasmania with his wife and children, drawing daily inspiration from family, faith, and the pursuit of meaningful impact.

As you turn this final page, remember — reinvention doesn't happen in isolation. It thrives in community, conversation, and continued reflection.
That's why I'd love to stay connected with you beyond this book — to keep sharing insights, encouragement, and real stories of growth as we each continue to evolve.

But before we do that, I have a small request to make.

A SMALL REQUEST

Thank you for reading *The Career Reinvention Blueprint™!*

I believe this book has the potential to transform thousands of lives — inspiring readers to move from *restless to realigned* and to rediscover purpose and possibility in their work and life.

Book reviews make an enormous difference. They help other readers discover this message and remind retailers that purpose-driven stories matter.

To help more people find this book, I'd love your support. Would you take a minute or two to leave an honest review with your favourite online bookstore — such as Amazon or Booktopia?

Every word you share means more than you know, and I read each one personally.

Simply scan the QR code below or visit www.careerreinventionblueprint.com/review

LET'S KEEP WALKING THIS PATH TOGETHER

Reinvention doesn't end with the last page; it's just the beginning of a deeper journey. I don't want this to be the end of our conversation.

➤ **Tell me your story**

I'd love to hear how this book spoke to you, the shifts you're making, or even the struggles you're still navigating. Write to me directly at david@davidonu.com.

➤ **Stay connected**

Join me on https://www.linkedin.com/in/drdavidonu, where I share honest reflections, lessons, and reminders to remind you that you're not walking alone.

➤ **Stay engaged**

Sign up for my **Grow and Love** newsletter at www.davidonu.com/grow-and-love, where I share more tools, encouragement, and grounded insights for your journey.

➤ **Personalised Coaching Support**

Occasionally, I open a few complimentary 30-minute Clarity Calls for readers ready to act on what they've discovered in this book. If that's you, share your reflections here:

I personally review each submission and will be in touch if there's a good fit.

Thank you for walking this journey with me.

Writing this book has been as much about my own growth as it is about yours. I hope you leave these pages with both clarity and courage – to take one small step toward alignment today.

You are not late, not behind, and not alone. You are right on time. You're not starting over – you're beginning aligned. And alignment changes everything.

Your next chapter is already waiting; it just needs you to take the next step. Remember, life rewards action.

As one of my guiding principles reminds me:

> *"We are all visitors to this time, this place. We are just passing through. Our purpose here is to observe, to learn, to grow, to love…and then we return home."*
>
> *– Australian Aboriginal proverb*

Here's to your reinvention journey and to the next chapter. See you soon!

BONUS: QUOTES TO INSPIRE YOUR REINVENTION JOURNEY

Because some days will be more challenging than others, here are words to keep close to your heart. Write them down. Stick them on your mirror. Carry them in your journal. Let them remind you of what's possible.

> *Sometimes the most respected paths are the ones that feel most restrictive. And the very identity that built your success can quietly become the box that traps you.*
>
> – Dr David Onu

> *I realize now that life is short, and we are very foolish if we do not keep a balance between work and family. If in trying to be a success, you lose your wife and family, you've lost it all.*
>
> – Gary Chapman

> *Doors don't open before you move – they open because you moved. So, you've got to make the bold move. It's only then that you see the next door.*
>
> – Dr David Onu

> *Awareness is the first step for meaningful transformation.*
>
> – Dr David Onu

Reinvention doesn't start with a resume. It begins with reflection. So, this is an invitation to pause, reflect, and realign with what truly matters.

– Dr David Onu

Before you can REALIGN, you must recognize where you've MISALIGNED. Before you pivot, you must recognize that you're stuck. And before you REINVENT, you must become deeply honest about WHAT NO LONGER FITS.

– Dr David Onu

Do not shrink to fit into the tiny perspex boxes others have prepared for you. Instead, be eager to expand to your higher purpose.

– Dr David Onu

Growth happens when you give yourself permission to step beyond the walls that once held you back.

– Dr David Onu

Your discontent is not disloyalty. It may be destiny knocking.

– Dr David Onu

Your mind is your most powerful tool. When you learn to train it right, you hold the key to a career – and a life – that fits you.

– Dr David Onu

Reinvention isn't betrayal. It's about alignment, not obligation.

— Dr David Onu

The cage called comfort is still a cage.

— Unknown

You're not starting over – you're starting aligned. And alignment is a game changer.

— Dr David Onu

You are not behind. You are right on time. You are more than ready.

— Dr David Onu

Your career can be a gift to your lineage, not just a badge for it.

— Dr David Onu

www.ingramcontent.com/pod-product-compliance
Lightning Source LLC
Chambersburg PA
CBHW020531080526
44583CB00013B/818